Praise for
Souls Speak

"I'm rattled to the core. This is an incredible true story; spooky, chilling, most definitely jaw-on-the-floor compelling. The author's investigative prowess and candid transparency will give even the staunchest skeptic reason to seriously consider the astonishing discoveries examined in this book. These paranormal events are mind-bending, unforgettable and not readily explained in any other way. Read this book!"

—Mary Beth Maas, Omaha reviewer

"A shocking paranormal twist to a historic missing childrens case. Riveting!"

—Steve Sederwall, Cold West Detective Agency

"I couldn't put this book down. A real page-turner!"

—Gary Lindberg, author, *Letters from Elvis*

Souls Speak

*missing children reveal their
serial killer from beyond*

Wisdom
Editions

Minneapolis

FIRST EDITION JULY 2019

Printed in the United States of America.

10 9 8 7 6 5 4 3 2 1

Cover and interior design: Gary Lindberg

ISBN: 978-1-950743-05-6

In memorium

Joel Hoag

Billy Hoag

Craig Dowell

Dedicated to the truth-seekers.
And to my family, whose prayers and faithful support
sustained me through this most surreal and
challenging investigation.

The important thing is not to stop questioning. Curiosity has its own reason for existence. One cannot help but be in awe when he contemplates the mysteries of eternity, of life, of the marvelous structure of reality.

Albert Einstein, theoretical physicist

God opposes our involvement in the occult because it belittles God and exalts man. Or to put it another way, the occult is simply a continuation of the ancient satanic deception in Genesis 3:5: "Go beyond what God has appointed, and you shall become like God." All forms of the occult present us with a similar temptation: will we act like humble children of the heavenly Father and submit to God's wisdom in limiting our knowledge and power, or will we, like Adam and Eve, hanker for the fruit that can make us "wise" and for the power that belongs to God? Will we belittle God and exalt ourselves, or will we humble ourselves and exalt God by being content with his revelation and his use of power on our behalf?

John Piper, theologian

The universe is made up of stories, not atoms.

Muriel Rukeyser, poet

Table of Contents

Also by John Wingate

Lost Boys of Hannibal
Inside America's Largest Cave Search

Souls Speak

*missing children reveal their
serial killer from beyond*

John Wingate

Minneapolis, Minnesota

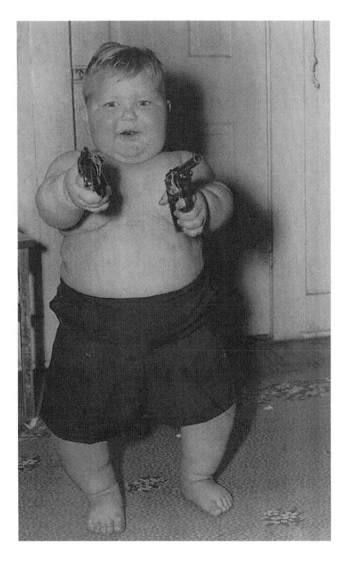

Serial killer John Wayne Gacy at age three (provided photo.)

Chapter 1
Most Bizarre

When I began this investigation, I thought everything that could be written about John Wayne Gacy had already been written. I was wrong. I was astonished to discover this evil and depraved man could intersect my own childhood in such a bizarre and chilling way. The information contained within these pages is mind-blowing.

To ponder the possibility that this monster could have abducted, sexually molested, strangled and buried friends of mine, more than half a century ago, is difficult to fathom. As adults we understand that death is a part of life, but in childhood we are never prepared for the death of young friends. It seems so foreign and impossible when our buddies are taken. Life is just beginning. When a loss is so sudden and unexpected, the shock is overwhelming. Grief follows with its component parts—sadness, heartache and emptiness. After more than fifty years, those feelings are still felt by two beleaguered families and many thousands of friends and others who have a warm affection and empathy for the memories of the three boys in this story.

Even after the passage of so many years, the grieving is not over. Let's begin.

* * *

John Wayne Gacy came into this world, chubby and screaming, on March 17, 1942—St. Patrick's Day. He was the second of three children, the only boy, born to Marion Elaine Robinson-Gacy and John Stanley Gacy. He was named after a famous Irishman, Hollywood star John Wayne, but young John—born of polish descent—would enjoy little Irish luck during his bittersweet childhood.

Devoted and adoring to his mother and sisters, Gacy failed to ever achieve a warm relationship with his stern alcoholic father. The familial dysfunction helped to create the man, self-described as a good Catholic, who had no hope of eternal salvation as he morphed into one of the most monstrous serial killers in US history.

A man brimming with contradictions, Gacy's life unfolded in Chicago, Illinois; Las Vegas, Nevada; Springfield, Illinois; and Waterloo, Iowa. He made friends easily and was viewed as outgoing, helpful and even brilliant. His popular backyard barbecues would attract scores of friends and associates. He would don full clown attire and entertain at birthday parties, the excited children clamoring for a hug from the stocky Pogo the Clown's big, strong arms. Yes, chilling to ponder.

But his dark nature was the flip side of this enigmatic character. It seems unimaginable that a human being could carry out the depraved acts Gacy administered to his thirty-three young male victims in the Chicago area during the 1970s. He was a dark wanderer in the night, cruising Cook County streets for male prostitutes or others willing to accept a ride to discuss a job opportunity or to get high before the night ended in torture, sodomy, slow strangulation and death. These demonic dramas were enacted in Gacy's own garage, even as his second wife slept soundly inside the house.

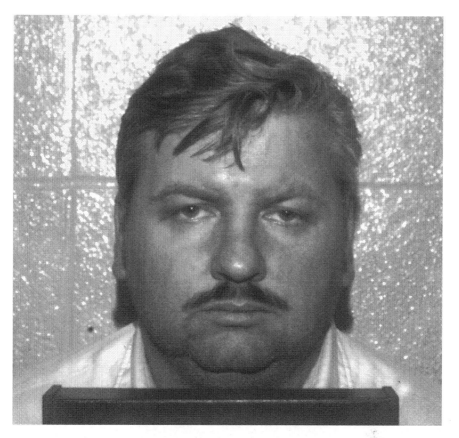

John Wayne Gacy mug shot, December 1978.
Des Plaines, Illinois Police Department

Most of the bodies were tossed like sacks of potatoes into the crawl space beneath his modest ranch home in Norwood Park Township, in the northwest Chicago suburbs. Gacy sprinkled his kills with lime to speed decomposition and diminish the odor, a dark and perverse anointing ritual before he buried them. And always one with an eye for detail, the twisted madman would methodically update his hand-drawn map showing precisely where each body was entombed in the dank earth below.

Equally unimaginable is the possibility that the life of this depraved and evil killer could intersect one of America's most vexing mysteries, a Missouri child disappearance case that began in May 1967 in historic Hannibal, a quaint town of twenty thousand souls known worldwide as the boyhood home of great American author Samuel Clemens who penned many classics as Mark Twain.

Historic Hannibal, Missouri. Photo courtesy George E. Walley Jr.

When three modern-day Tom Sawyers vanished after exploring a network of newly-discovered caves, exposed during major road construction, the disappearance birthed the largest cave search in US history. Despite a month-long search by more than one hundred experienced cavers and hundreds of other volunteers, the boys were never found. The pastoral town of Hannibal, nestled along the Mississippi River in northeast Missouri, never fully recovered from the calamity. The event marked the only time in US caving history the parties being sought were not found.

Today, fifty-two years later, we still mourn Joel Hoag, thirteen, his eleven-year-old brother Billy, and their neighbor Edwin Craig Dowell, fourteen. For these many decades, the conventional wisdom has been that the boys were lost in the caves, perhaps victims of a calamitous ceiling collapse that the cavers were unable to find among the impossibly complex labyrinths inside the maze caves.

Astounding New Developments

A most astonishing series of events began to unfold during the late spring and summer of 2018 that fingered John Wayne Gacy as the abductor and killer of the Hoag and Dowell boys. Equally astounding are the sources of this shocking revelation. Identical stories were told to me by three women intuitive mediums, two in Missouri and one living on a ranch in the state of Wyoming. Within a two-month period, these women independently had visions of the boys' abductions and murders by Gacy. This information, they explained, was sensed as they channeled the immaterial vibrational energy from the other side in contacts with the etheric spirit of Gacy and the spirits of the missing and long-deceased boys.

In addition, these women believe the boys' murders were likely Gacy's first kills, five full years before his murderous spree even began in suburban Chicago. Gacy would have been only twenty-five at the time, barely a man himself. Yet, the Waterloo, Iowa, restaurant manager, married with two small children, was already steeped in a lustful evil that could be sated only by the torture and killing of innocent young boys, true innocents who were denied their lives for simply being in the wrong place at the wrong time.

These psychic sleuths are all sober-minded, responsible, self-described Christian women. Transgressing the veil between worlds, they peered across time and from beyond the chasm between this world and the spiritual realm of the heavenlies to reveal one of the most perplexing and unfathomable experiences of my life.

I didn't search out this story—it found me and rocked my reality. Being a committed Christian, I am skeptical of what the New Age has to offer, essentially anything *but* Christianity it seems. So, initially, it was difficult to fully accept the news from these sincere and credible women who quietly use their preternatural gifts for good. The three mediums focus on what they call their God-given gifts and shun most other practices in the New Age category. All three typically avoid publicity for their roles in missing persons and other police cases in the US. It was clear to me they weren't in this drama to capture any national attention. While they all greatly valued their privacy, the clairvoyants, all mothers, felt a strong commitment and a special empathy for the three boys and their families as they tried to bring resolution to this painful chapter in the lives of so many.

It's important to underscore the fact that these women came to the same conclusions completely independent of each other, something beyond coincidence as you'll likely agree. I interviewed the women carefully and separately. Their sincerity was obvious, and all three have reputations as honest people.

Incredibly, the more we investigated and discovered, the greater our confidence this trio of psychic mediums appeared to be correct in their assessment of what they had supernaturally experienced. It begged the question of whether, perhaps, this was an active move of God. Perhaps these women were divinely chosen to finally locate the lost boys of Hannibal and bring closure to the emotional pain and haunting mystery.

Still, being attentive and faithful to the Holy Bible's admonition about avoiding the unfathomable supernatural realm with its dark mysteries, I cautiously persisted as an observer, exploring whether these fantastic disclosures might be nothing more than a huge evil deception. Were their disclosures the dark fruits of fallen trickster spirits intent on fomenting more pain, sadness and despair after more than half a century of mystery about the boys' shared fate? After all, the demon spirits that infested John Wayne Gacy are eternal and know the facts of what happened. Could they fool these sincere mediums into believing they were communicating with the spirits of the boys and Gacy? Is their whole point to sow confusion and more emotional pain? After all, that's what demons do—they act in opposition to God's love and Divine plans as they have for millennia, disrupting and destroying lives.

If what these psychic mediums have channeled is true, Gacy was killing much earlier than police previously thought. In fact, our remarkable investigation found that John Gacy's dark nature was quite evolved as early as age fifteen when he saw younger boys as sexual prey and threatened to kill them if they didn't cooperate. And he was most likely killing far beyond Cook County, Illinois as he traveled extensively. In fact, as our investigation unfolded beyond the Hoag and Dowell boys, two more northeast Missouri boys were identified as possible Gacy victims by one of the psychics.

Prepare yourself. This story is true, and I have described events exactly as they occurred. This journey will challenge your boundaries of reality and broaden your understanding of the nature of both good and evil, across the totality of God's impossibly complex creation. We pursue this paranormal story responsibly, in the hope of finding a single shared grave in heavily wooded Northeast Missouri, the very spot where these three psychic mediums believe the bodies of Joel, Billy, and Craig remain buried, awaiting discovery.

Chapter 2
The Unseen Realm

At twenty-eight, the young woman's life was in jeopardy as she lay in the hospital bed. Her name was Betty, now pregnant for the second time, but it was not going well. Although this pregnancy was five months along, the slender, petite woman wasn't even showing; her abdomen remained as flat as her bedside tabletop.

Betty was very ill, unable to keep down any food. The thought of drinking milk for its vital nutrients turned her stomach. "No way," she told the hospital staff.

Doctors said she was having an allergic reaction to the fetal life within. Today, they have a treatment to prevent this serious complication. But in the 1950s, Betty was on her own as two lives hung in the balance. Doctors prepared her, explaining their best option may be to remove the fetus in order to save Betty's life. After sharing the sobering news, they left the room, promising to return in the morning with an update on her condition.

Battling nausea and terrible despair, the young woman lay in bed tossing and turning as rain and sleet came in waves against the windows, which were incessantly rattling from the March wind and near-constant thunder. As dusk turned to darkness, sleep seemed her only option for escape from this painful situation. But first, Betty fixed her eyes upon the simple wooden crucifix hanging on the far wall, put aside her fear and hopelessness, and whispered a simple prayer: "Jesus, please save my baby."

Suddenly, the veil between heaven and earth separated. Betty startled as a golden glow outlined the crucifix and began to expand until it engulfed her petite frame. The fear and anxiety she had felt was now gone, replaced by a perfect peace that filled her being. Although momentarily stunned by what was happening, Betty's eyes finally surrendered to overwhelming fatigue, and she slid into a deep sleep.

The next morning, Betty awoke at dawn feeling stronger and clear-headed. The window-rattling storm had passed, and the sun was climbing in the eastern sky. She noticed she felt much better; the nausea was finally gone, replaced now by a gnawing, ravenous hunger. She called for the nurse's aide and asked for a tall glass of cold milk. She drank it right down and asked for another. Then, she enjoyed a hearty hospital breakfast, her first real meal in days.

The doctors and nurses were perplexed, at a loss to explain this sudden recovery from such a life-threatening illness. Despite being terribly ill for many days, it appeared Betty was now perfectly healthy. "What happened overnight?" her doctor asked. "I don't know, her vitals are normal now," replied the nurse. "She slept peacefully and didn't stir." The hospital staff was mystified by what had transpired in room 217 at Levering Hospital. How could someone so sick be healed literally overnight?

But Betty understood; the Great Physician had paid a visit. Her simple, heartfelt prayer had been heard and answered.

Discharged from the hospital, Betty returned home to her husband and five-year-old daughter. The medical emergency was behind her, but something remarkable was happening.

While she'd shown no visual evidence of being pregnant before, her abdomen was finally growing, revealing the developing life within, now seemingly on an accelerated schedule at month five of this difficult pregnancy. Four months later, Betty gave birth to a perfectly healthy eight-pound boy. They named him John.

Even today, it is a profound revelation to ponder this story. You see, Betty is my mother, now age ninety-four and blessed with longevity. I exist because of her faithfulness when all seemed impossibly dark and hopeless. At age seven, when I was first told this story, I discovered Jesus was real in a deep and profoundly personal way. He had saved me in the womb.

Remarkable manifestations such as what my mother experienced happen around us daily. They are cataloged in our minds as Divine miracles, visions, coincidences, oddities or dreams. We often struggle to wrap our minds around these events because of the limitations of our human mind. Truth is, we journey through life seeing reality only fractionally, unable to fully witness its unfathomable depths of intricacies and complexities. Truly, God's infinite creation is beyond the grasp of our three-pound brain.

Occasionally, our reality intersects at a place where the material world, locked into the constraints of clocks and calendars, and only three dimensions, gives way to a place beyond space and time. This is a place of energy and vibration where mortality eventually ends and births our energetic souls into an etheric, non-physical realm.

The individuals who explore this boundary between our world and the realm beyond are called by a variety of terms— clairvoyants, intuitive mediums or psychics. They claim to connect with spirit energy on the other side and bring back information they assert can heal broken relationships, provide comfort to a grieving family member, locate missing persons and even solve crimes.

What do we know about this strange non-physical realm?

Christian believers celebrate heaven, our eternal resting place where the Creator Triune God ordains our energetic spirit or soul to rest in a joyful, perfect peace for eternity, free of earthly worry, struggle and pain. But there are other realms too, occupied by dark spirits and demons, the fallen angels, where confusion, deception and despairing psychological pain are the goals of these tormentors. They are always at odds with God's important work, battling against His goodness and truth.

Ephesians 6:12 tells of the "heavenly places," a realm beyond our mortal world where these spiritual entities exist with their own minds, wills and emotions. Theologians believe they are in league with Satan who, along with a third of the angels, were cast out of heaven after rebelling against God. These deceiving spirits convince people that suicide is a good solution to their troubles. They persuade people that behaviors cannot be sinful if they fulfill our needs and seem right and enjoyable from our own selfish human perspective. And they smoothly convince young people that satanic music is just part of the modern scene and harmless entertainment or a counter-culture mantra.

While the supernatural New Age is popular in our culture, make no mistake, we are engaged in a spiritual battle, as old as humanity itself, between two opposing kingdoms. And as Christians, we have access to the protection of the only being Satan has never defeated—Jesus.

These "heavenly places" are not heaven. Christian theologians believe mediums, occultists and New Age worshipers are likely communicating with spirits in the heavenlies, not heaven. That's why Jesus, in Matthew 6:9, teaches believers to direct their prayers: "This, then, is how you should pray: 'Our Father *in heaven*, hallowed be your name...'"

The paranormal environment, which is as real as the world we see with our earthly eyes, can be very deceiving and dangerous, according to church leaders, as the following story demonstrates.

Dangerous Demonic Oppression

Pastor Rob Cunningham (not his real name), now retired, formerly led one of the largest evangelical mega-churches in Minneapolis-St. Paul. Periodically, he would include in his sermon, as a teaching moment, a true story about an encounter with the darkness found in the supernatural realm. One especially chilling story he shared on a Sunday morning has been impossible for me to forget, despite the passage of several years.

Stephen, seventeen, was deep into the goth movement. He dressed in black and listened to dark music with chilling satanic lyrics. The boy would spend most of his time in his room, the music bouncing off the four walls papered with creepy posters. Stephen had made this movement, this music, his god and he worshipped it.

The high strangeness ratcheted up when Stephen's mother called Pastor Rob with a desperate plea. "Pastor Rob, you have to come over. Strange things are happening, and I need help with Stephen," she exclaimed. Pastor Rob quickly drove to the family's home, not quite knowing what to expect. When he was welcomed inside, he noticed all of the lights in the house were flashing off and on, and satanic music was blaring from Stephen's upstairs bedroom. The cacophony was mind-numbing. The deafening clatter from an old window air conditioner only added to the chaos, as the mother frantically chattered on trying to get answers about what was happening.

Wanting to reduce the noise level, Pastor Rob walked over to the air conditioner and pulled the cord from the power outlet. He was stunned. A chill raced up his spine, as the air conditioner continued to operate without benefit of electrical power. The pastor quickly recognized they were caught up in an unfolding demonic event. He walked through every room praying the blood of Jesus and binding and casting out any demonic oppressions that were busily at work around this poor family. Soon, the lights in the house stopped flashing off and on, and the noisy air conditioner fell silent. Pastor Rob even coaxed Stephen from his room and tried to talk to him, but the troubled boy would have none of it and fled the house.

After calming the mother, Pastor Rob returned to the church, still concerned about the bizarre encounter. He thought it was like a strange and dark gothic novel, as he played the events over and over in his mind. The three of them had been ill-fated characters being victimized by harassing malicious spirits.

Two hours later, Stephen's mother called again, "Pastor Rob, it's happening again!" The pastor explained that as a believer she could pray to clear the house just as he had done. Still, he sensed something more, so he returned to the house. After praying again, the house grew silent. Then, he noticed Stephen standing out by the street.

Pastor Rob opened the front door and encouraged the boy to come inside so they could talk.

"I can't," cried the boy.

"Yes, you can," Pastor Rob replied. "Just come in, and we'll pray together."

"No, you don't understand," Stephen yelled. "They won't let me!"

Stephen was being physically restrained, supernaturally, so he was unable to approach Pastor Rob, a strong believer reflecting God's light into this very dark and evil circumstance. It was like an invisible supernatural force field intersected the front yard, keeping the boy from getting any closer to his mother and the pastor.

This story ended badly, as Stephen again rejected God and the offer of prayerful Divine protection. The troubled teen ran away and jumped from a high bridge taking his own life.

The choice of death over life is the antithesis of what flows from the Creator God. All that God touches brings and honors life: it is His will that we live until we are called home to Heaven. Stephen's demons from the supernatural heavenlies had sadly convinced him suicide was the best and only solution.

* * *

The Holy Bible, in the Old Testament book of Deuteronomy, warns us to avoid this dark realm where lying, deceiving, demonic entities can skillfully masquerade as beings of light and truth-tellers to gain a foothold in someone's life. Most people lack the experience and extreme discernment required to identify good intentions from evil deception across this boundary between earth and the unknowable realm; that's why pastors say it's best to just leave it alone and give it wide berth.

Supernatural Sleuths

Still, the story detailed in *Souls Speak* challenges all we know about what lies beyond our world in this mysterious supernatural realm. We wonder whether God is at work in a remarkable way that we cannot fully fathom. This story appears a great mystery, so what do we do with it? Do we believe it or dismiss the whole scenario? Humans often fear the unknown, so shall we be afraid to go forth and explore this remarkable series of supernatural events?

We know God spoke all of creation into existence, and He continues to speak into that existence, our reality, even today. But should we believe everything that appears miraculous without imposing it to scrutiny and critical biblical perspective? Of course not; thus we have chosen to pursue these events through the lens of a Christian worldview, allowing the readers to see both sides of this extraordinary investigation. My hope is that you come away with a better understanding of the impossibly complex tapestry of God's creation we experience during our material and mortal existence, and thereafter.

We also must ask whether this could be the work of magic and mere wishes, worthy of being abandoned by critical, discerning minds? On the other hand, if this is true, it would be scandalous to not give the subject the considerable inquiry it requires. In the end, we must ask ourselves whether the Creator of all things is communicating with three perceptive women who independently validate and corroborate the identical information about the fate of three children long thought lost in the caves.

The three American intuitive mediums in *Souls Speak* are young women ranging in age from twenty-six to thirty-one, living hundreds of miles apart. They shared their remarkably similar stories from beyond with me during the second half of 2018. All three psychics report they pray to God for protection and guidance when they are connecting with the spirit world. They often use their intuitive gifts to help other people by offering information that may be helpful for the challenging circumstances they face.

What these psychic sleuths sensed and experienced—if ultimately true—would profoundly rewrite this most vexing US mystery, the sudden 1967 disappearance of the Hoag and Dowell boys in historic Hannibal, billed in the tourism trade as *America's Hometown,* which welcomes more than three hundred thousand visitors annually.

During the span of this investigation, the women reportedly connected with the spiritual energy of these deceased boys as they named their serial killer, John Wayne Gacy. The trio of mediums revealed the boys' torture and murders in chilling detail and then identified the precise piece of wooded real estate in Northeast Missouri where they believe the three victims still share a shallow grave, a brief drive from where they were last seen. And Gacy even confessed the murders, baiting one of the psychics with an arrogant challenge, "You'll never find them."

These women divulged this astonishing information during independent channeling sessions and three separate driving tours with me in the Hannibal area during August and September 2018. What transpired as this shocking and bizarre story unfolded rattled my world and the lives of the victims' loved ones.

After hearing their stories, I privately hoped these psychic women were being lifted up to do a powerful work for good, to finally end the pain and bring closure to the terrible mystery of Hannibal's three lost boys. Or, was this nothing more than a cruel trick by deceiving, demonic spirits, as we'll explore in a later chapter.

We continue our journey by visiting one of these psychic sleuths in northeastern Wyoming.

Mary Riley, twenty-six, slides her left foot into the stirrup and launches herself onto the friendly mare for a quick ride down the lane to get the day's mail. Mary lives on a ranch with her husband and three children in northeastern Wyoming, about a one-hour drive from the South Dakota border.

This corner of the American West is populated by spectacular mountain vistas, clear streams and rivers, and open plains for the Riley's grazing cattle herd and horses. Plenty of breathing room here in Big Sky country. The Riley's love life here, a salt-of-the-earth family that trusts in the Lord and embraces the self-reliant values that helped build their four-generation ranching operation here in God's country.

The blonde, blue-eyed Mary has a special gift, first discovered at age four while playing in her grandmother's backyard. The happy preschooler glanced up from her toys to see a tall man, a stranger to her, suddenly appear a few feet away. "He was wearing a tan cowboy hat, button-up shirt and rounded-toe cowboy boots. He had no beard, but seemed older because his face was wrinkled," Mary recalled, the incident still crystal clear in her mind more than two decades later.

Startled, young Mary bolted to the house and into the comfort of her grandmother's arms. When Mary described the man she'd seen in the yard, her grandmother pulled a photo album from the top shelf of a closet and thumbed through the pages until she found the photo she sought. Pointing to the photo, she asked Mary, "Is this the man you saw?" Mary replied the figure in the photo was indeed the one she had seen in the backyard moments earlier.

Mary had seen her great grandfather, who had died decades before she was born. It was a stunning revelation for the child, too young to fully comprehend the paranormal experience. During the ensuing years, Mary slowly grew to realize this natural gift to see what others could not, things beyond this present-day world, was an amazing ability she could neither fully explain nor understand. While Mary's mother discouraged her from giving too much attention to this supernatural talent, Mary later realized during high school that if this was a gift from God, and she believed it was, then she wanted to use this ability to help others.

While growing up, Mary found herself drawn to abandoned places where she sensed the energies from the past. She explained, "Many rundown places are like that because they're full of negative energy. People don't like living around this energy, so in time the place falls into disrepair and is abandoned. Had they brought in a pastor or minister to bless the location, it would have resolved the issues and been fine."

Mary often has used her intuitive talents to aid worried families looking for missing persons. In May 2018, she helped an Austin, Texas family find a daughter who had run away from home, joining the hundreds of thousands of teens who become runaways annually across America. In early June, Mary sensed the family would find the girl three weeks later, specifically on July third, in the small town where she was born—and they did, just as she had predicted.

On January 16, 2018, a Spearfish, South Dakota man, Christopher Oien, twenty-eight, was reported missing after a weekend of gambling and partying in Deadwood, South Dakota. Authorities knew it would be difficult to find him; they were enduring a harsh winter with deep snow and more falling all the time across the region. Once Mary began to focus on the case, she passed along all she sensed to a detective on the case. "I told him they would find the missing man's hat by a dumpster on a backstreet of Deadwood. A few weeks later, they found his hat by a dumpster on a back street," Mary explained.

Mary had further visions about his condition and whereabouts. "He died of hypothermia. I felt he was very cold—his legs were so cold. He's in a wooded area on the side of a steep hill." She told police they would find him in twelve weeks.

Authorities continued to maintain an intense search for the man, utilizing horseback riders and aerial drones, without success. Finally, a man hunting for deer antlers stumbled upon Oien's body in a steep, rugged area near Deadwood. It was early April, twelve weeks after his disappearance, just as Mary had predicted.

In July 2018, Mary read a newspaper account I provided about Mollie Tibbetts, twenty, who had vanished after jogging in the small town of Brooklyn, Iowa, a rural burb fifty miles west of Iowa City where she attended college.

A few minutes after reading the article she had a clairvoyant vision. "I am picking up on a Hispanic male in his twenties, dark complexion, dark hair and a silver watch with diamonds in it. I hear the word Texas and see a black vehicle," Mary said.

Mary then drops a terrifying bombshell that shakes the night, unsure if the information is related to the Tibbetts case or another one. "I see this happening in more than just Iowa, and I see [the victims] on an auction or bidding site." Mary has psychically identified what appears to be a trafficking ring that is marketing and selling human beings, perhaps on the Dark Web, a secretive, unholy realm of the Internet where criminals lurk and transact in the illegal currencies of drugs and human beings.

Stunned by the specificity of Mary's vision, I quickly email the information to Poweshiek County Iowa investigators. A month later, Tibbetts' body is found decomposing in a cornfield only a few miles from her home. An undocumented Hispanic man in his twenties, who worked nearby as a farmhand, was soon arrested and charged. He drove a black vehicle and had come to the US as a child through Texas.

While many psychics see only glimpses of people or events, Mary apparently is able to see detailed scenes much like a series of photographs spread out on a table. "When I see something it's like I'm looking down this tunnel. The center is clear, and it gets blurry and darker toward the edges." Mary is able to see people, locations and situations with her eyes open or closed, frequently choosing to close her eyes for greater concentration.

For years, she had little control over this ability, often sensing things about other people at the grocery store or mall. Now, in early adulthood, she tries to control and steer her psychic focus with some success.

A private person, Mary dislikes drawing attention to this supernatural gift. A faithful Christian, she is solely focused on doing good to help other people. "When I was younger, I struggled with this ability and fell into a depression for a short time," Mary said. "I read the Bible, and it says not to treat a medium as God, and I thought how could anyone do that? I want people to *know* God." In time, Mary grew to see her intuitive ability differently. "God gave me this gift, and I've never been so close to Him as I am now. Never would I go against God. I want to do good."

Before Mary channels a person or situation, peering into another realm where space-time is different, she prays. "I ask God for guidance and protection because I can see terrible things, and the energy is not always good. It can be unsettling and exhausting," she explains.

So, comfortable with her gift, Mary bravely goes forward to face what comes, confident God is with her and can use all things for His good, as revealed in a favorite scripture: *And we know that in all things, God works for the good of those who love him, who have been called according to his purpose* (Romans 8:28 NIV).

* * *

We travel back to the year 2013. Mary, then twenty, is in Denver, Colorado, relaxing while visiting one of her sisters. One sunny afternoon they are strolling through a gentrified neighborhood and perusing the various gift and antique shops populating this section of Denver's inner city. The tinkling doorbell announces Mary as she enters a dusty, cluttered shop with lots of antiques and knickknacks to explore.

"I was looking around and spotted this clown photograph on a shelf. When I picked it up, I immediately felt very uneasy. There was a lot of energy associated with it, and a chilling feeling went through me. The photo literally felt cold in my hands." Perplexed, Mary decided to buy the photo, holding it up for the store clerk to see. "Oh, that's not for sale. It's the owner's photo of Gacy," the clerk responded.

The moment was electric as negative energy pulsed through Mary's body. The image was that of John Wayne Gacy, the depraved psychopath who regularly portrayed the character Pogo the clown, entertaining children at birthday parties in his native Chicago. But his true, dark and demonic nature lurked beneath the colorful costume and greasepaint seen in the photograph Mary now held in her hands.

John Wayne Gacy, among America's most notorious serial killers, was executed on May 10, 1994, twenty-seven years to the day after the Hannibal boys went missing, an interesting coincidence of the calendar. Gacy buried twenty-six of his thirty-three victims in a crawl space beneath his suburban Norwood Park Township ranch home in Cook County, Illinois. Three other victims were buried on his property, while the other four were disposed of in the nearby Des Plaines River. Gacy's first known victim was stabbed to death, but the rest were tortured, raped and murdered by asphyxiation or strangulation with a tourniquet he made from a length of rope and a pipe. He was the worst kind of human being, a pedophile with an insatiable and uncontrollable rage that drove him to torture and kill.

As a millennial born two decades after Gacy's reign of terror, Mary knew nothing about the accomplished killer, recalling only his name being mentioned as part of a psychology class lesson in high school years earlier. Mary was shaken but intrigued. Why had she experienced such a strong reaction to this Gacy photograph? Was this a nudge from beyond to dig deeper? Did this depraved killer have something to reveal to her from beyond the grave? Was this merely the first signpost on a mind-blowing journey of profound significance? Mary's extraordinary experience in the antique shop foreshadowed the terrifying visions she would psychically experience during the summer of 2018—and the news would rock the world.

Chapter 3
Genesis of a Mystery

When I was a boy, I'd visit a rock quarry at the end of the street where we lived in Hannibal. I'd hike across my friend David Brooks' backyard and stand atop the hundred-foot-high cliff, taking in the sweeping view of the quarry below. There were no warning signs or fences to keep curious children away; the high cliff's edge suddenly revealed itself as the grassy backyard ended, just beyond the Brooks family's prolific garden.

To the north and south of the clifftop, sloping, well-used trails led down into the quarry. Beyond, less than a quarter mile away, the glittering Mississippi River flowed past as it had for eons, a picture postcard backdrop for this idyllic boyhood oasis.

Long ago, Burlington Limestone was quarried at this site, blasted from the face and taken in huge quantities by rail for production of cement and construction blocks. The quarrying activity at this location had ended more than a century ago, but the vast plain remained an inviting and wild playground for generations of neighborhood kids.

On carefree afternoons, we'd portray brave, adventurous soldiers or cowboys, look for fossils, or pluck garter snakes from the exposed rocky overhangs along the edges of the cirque and the dense woodlands surrounding the quarry. Sometimes, we'd make historic finds, retrieving our pocket knives to excavate civil war era musket balls from the cliff face.

Rock quarry atop the Murphy's Cave bluff on Hannibal's southside.

At the far eastern edge of the quarry, just before the tree line, sat a massive granite boulder the size of a small school bus, one end higher than the other, pointing skyward. This geological erratic—out of place amidst all this limestone—was deposited here by the sweeping fingers of a glacier that sculpted the northeast Missouri terrain millions of years ago.

My friends and I would scramble up the boulder, plop down at its highest point and soak up the warmth from the sunbaked granite. Here, we would drink from our Cub Scout canteens, eat apples or pears scavenged from a neighbor's trees, ponder big ideas and hatch plans for future adventures.

What I didn't know during those carefree days of childhood, as we sat on our massive boulder, was that a remarkable subterranean world lay below us, tucked away in the eons-old Louisiana Limestone. Ironically, this cave system was completely unknown to the younger children in the neighborhood. But that would change in a few years, once the cave network became ground zero for a haunting, traumatic event in the lives of many people.

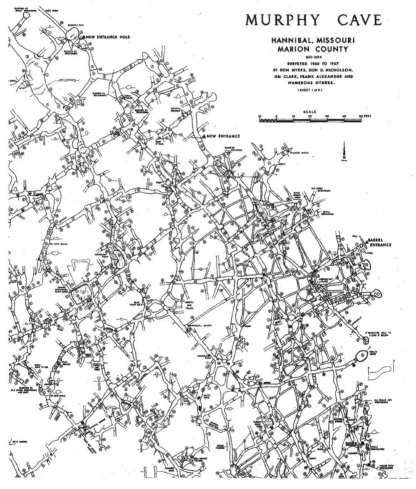

A portion of the Murphy's Cave Map. Courtesy Missouri Speleological Survey.

This vast labyrinth of crisscrossed cave passages, many coffin-snug, has a chilly year-round temperature of fifty-two degrees. Locally, it is known as Murphy's Cave, one of the region's most complex maze caves. The cave was first discovered in 1873 by workmen digging for fire clay and promptly named after Cornelius Murphy, the landowner at the time, who operated a small grocery store at the corner of Birch and Walnut streets, adjacent to the high hill containing the cave system.

In April of that year, five children ages nine to thirteen decided to enter an exposed entrance and explore the cave. Soon, the youngsters were impossibly lost, and to complicate matters the youngest boy began to feel the effects of hypothermia in his spare frame.

By late evening, word of the missing children made its way to the parents who had been wondering about their whereabouts all evening. The alarm fueled a vast crowd outside the cave entrance. About eleven o'clock, a search party of five men filled oil lanterns and entered the dark cave, making their way slowly through the precarious passageways. In some passages they could stand, but usually the cavers were hunched over or on their hands and knees, crawling through the tighter routes.

After searching for an hour, joy overtook the terrible worry when the men heard a young voice exclaim, "Oh, I see a light!" The lost children were soon found, tucked away in a large intersection of passages in the chilly limestone, their bodies pressed together to stay warm. By one o'clock, the rescuers and the rescued emerged into the night to cries of joy as parents hugged their children, eyes streaming with tears, their lips quietly uttering prayers of thanksgiving to God for safe deliverance.

The Hannibal newspaper put out a special edition on the caving calamity giving citizens their first sense of this new-found cave. "The avenues are said to be very narrow and torturous. They intersect each other after the manner of streets and blocks," reported the *Hannibal Courier* newspaper. The

Murphy's Cave entrance was closed, but it would be ground zero again nearly a century later.

The lesson learned in 1873 was a sobering one for parents and children to heed—caves are dangerous and should be avoided by untrained and ill-equipped explorers.

But boys being boys, another group of young teens had their lust for adventure override any sense of caution on a beautiful summer day in June 1961. Ed Owen, sixteen, and his brother Ron, a year younger, gleefully discovered a cave opening into Murphy's located less than a block from the Owen family's Birch Street home.

The boys scampered up into the weeds and found the opening plugged with a fifty-five-gallon barrel. They put hands to rusty steel and wrenched the barrel out of the opening. One by one, the Owen teens and two friends dropped down into the vertical opening and began exploring.

"Someone brought a big ball of heavy string, so we unfurled that as we proceeded," Ed explained. "We'd heard it was a confusing cave with lots of passages, so I knew the tendency to get lost would be great."

The boys moved cautiously forward, their sneakers scuffing the buff-colored clay silt. Each boy had a flashlight which they agreed to rotate to maximize their light in the inky darkness. After exploring several hundred feet of passages, going left, then right, then left again, the last length of string was spent. Unfortunately, the boys boldly continued, confident they could find their way back. They pushed onward for what seemed like hours, but Ron was growing cold, with anxiety and fear wracking his mind. Ed told him to sit down and stay put. "We'll be back shortly," he reassured his brother.

Ron settled in and sat alone in his dirty trousers, his back flush against the cool limestone wall. He had neither water nor food; his lone flashlight now emitted only a faint glow, so he kept it off most of the time. When he felt his anxiety growing, he would quickly turn on the light as a faint beacon in this terrible, suffocating darkness. Every fear welled up within his T-shirt-clad frame as the cold seeped deeper, robbing his core of life-giving warmth.

Ron had woefully discovered it is always midnight in a cave, a surreal world of complete and total darkness. He waved a hand in front of his face to test this inky environment, but it went unseen. In fact, sitting in this cramped passage, he couldn't tell whether his eyes were open or closed. "It was scary," Ron recalled. "I waited for three hours, maybe longer, in complete cave darkness. That is a lot of time when you're cold and alone in the dark."

Ron longed for Ed and their friends to return, certain he'd never find his way out alone in this terrible darkness. Ron's mood was full-on despair in the dark silence; his only companions were the sounds of his breathing and heartbeat.

Suddenly, after an interminable lull, he heard muted voices, followed by a flickering light, and he knew the others had returned to save him.

Blessed by good fortune and heartfelt, desperate prayers, the boys carefully retraced their steps, remembering landmarks and watching for their sneaker prints in the clay silt. In another hour, their hearts raced as their last failing flashlight illuminated the end of the string, their tether out of this terrible place.

"It was a gift from God that got us out of there," Ed explained years later, the memories still crystalline in his memory. "I've never seen such a maze cave. Those passages were all over, and we certainly didn't see all of it." In hindsight, the Owen brothers, now past retirement age, viewed their younger selves as foolish, impulsive boys, prone to act before thinking. "We were overly brave," Ed explained, "and so foolish to take the risk. I do think we could have died in there."

When I interviewed the Owen brothers, the distant traumatic memories came flooding back as if their subterranean adventure had happened only yesterday. Even now, Ron sleeps with a night-light, providing him a measure of comforting illumination through the darkness. The dark hours inside Murphy's Cave had taken a lasting toll. "The complete darkness, all alone, is a memory I'll never forget," said Ron.

Ed and Ron Owen by a sealed entrance to Murphy's Cave.
Photo by John Wingate

In the following years, several experienced Missouri cavers teamed together to map as much of Murphy's Cave as possible. Their labors contributed important speleological knowledge for Missouri, often called the Cave State with 7,400-plus caves identified and more being found all the time. When their speleological mapping work was completed in 1966, the cavers had explored two miles of complex passages in Murphy's Cave, at least the ones they managed to squeeze through. The remaining known passages were either full of breakdown rubble or too small for adults to maneuver. The long hours they spent carefully mapping this subterranean world beneath my childhood rock quarry above would prove to be prescient work.

* * *

In May 1967, a major highway construction project was underway to reroute State Highway 79 on Hannibal's southern edge, to create a new ribbon of highway to the St. Louis area. Birch Street, which runs past Murphy's Cave hill, was torn up as construction workers prepared to widen the busy roadway. Four blocks farther south, where Birch would become Highway 79, workmen had spent many days dynamiting a high, wooded hill, removing millions of tons of trees, rock and soil to create a straight path for the highway, a roadcut through the limestone.

The construction work revealed an entrance into Murphy's Cave that captured the interest of twentieth-century children. And farther south, at the roadcut, the site of the recent demolition, heavy equipment also scraped open the ceilings of several cave passages, part of a heretofore unknown cave network beneath Hannibal's southern edge. These complex maze passages that cavers would soon explore extended for more than a mile beneath the highway construction zone and the adjacent Lovers Leap hill, the three-hundred-foot-high overlook offering spectacular views of Hannibal, the Mississippi River and the rich Illinois farmland to the east.

Soon, both cave areas would be the focus of an extensive search after three curious boys vanished, catapulting Hannibal into the headlines worldwide.

Joel Hoag, thirteen, was a good friend of mine during elementary school at A. D. Stowell School. He was an inquisitive teen who loved to explore the hills near his home, located only a few blocks from the highway construction site. Joel loved science, especially astronomy and natural history. Like most children who grew up in the 1960s, Joel and I, along with the other kids in the neighborhood, frequently explored the hilly forests and high bluffs, building forts or looking for fossils and snakes. Occasionally, we would come upon a small cave opening in a hill or someone's backyard. Most of these passages didn't lead very far before becoming too small to accommodate a boy. Others were filled with debris from ceiling collapses over the centuries.

Joel's brother Billy, eleven, was always tagging along with the older boys, hungry for adventure. The good-natured fifth grader, with his red hair and blue eyes, enjoyed pulling pranks on his siblings and friends. The Hoag boys came from a family of thirteen. Parents Mike and Helen raised eleven children, and it seemed most everyone in town knew them. Mike ran a popular family-friendly tavern on North Main known for its tamales, meatloaf and homemade pies.

The Hoag boys' friend Edwin Craig Dowell, fourteen, lived at 600 Union Street directly behind the Hoag home on Fulton Avenue. Craig, as he was called by friends, was an easy-going teen who liked pullover sweaters and wingtip shoes, popular teen garb in the late 1960s. Craig enjoyed tinkering with bicycles and was a curious, inquisitive young man, according to friends.

The Hoag boys and their playmates loved the outdoors and were already making plans for another summer of exploration among the Southside's forested hills and bluffs. Hannibal's lush countryside was a second home for them when the weather cooperated. The boys found real adventures like they had read about in their well-worn copies of Mark Twain's *Adventures of Tom Sawyer.*

Joel, Craig and Billy were especially excited about the massive Highway 79 road construction project nearby. They loved watching the construction crews manning huge belching earthmovers and shovels as they did dangerous work. Loud booms were heard for a few weeks as the crew dynamited rock and soil to transform the once-forested hills into a modern scenic highway corridor.

The trio made an exciting discovery the afternoon of Monday, May 8. As they watched the road construction activity from their high perch on the rocky, sloped roadcut, they noticed the demolition and the earthmover's blades had uncovered several limestone cave openings, entry points into the previously unknown labyrinth of complex subterranean passages.

"Look at that!" Joel said, pointing down to one of the roadbed openings. The boys quickly departed for the Hoag house where they fashioned a crude ladder to ease their entry into the beckoning cave openings.

As the boys descended through the dust cloud into one of the cave openings, their eyes adjusted to the thick darkness cut by their flashlight. Their heads swiveled around as they got their first look at an amazing subterranean world. The mayhem from the large earthmovers overhead now sounded muffled and distant. Joel swung the flashlight around and found the cave passages dry, spreading out in many directions like tentacles. In spots, the cave's ceiling was at least twice their height, the passages up to six feet wide. "This is amazing," one of the boys surely exclaimed as the trio absorbed the cave's grandeur.

They proceeded slowly, often coming to other passages that were barely large enough to squeeze through. The air smelled dusty and stale. As the boys walked along, dust and small bits of rock rained down on them from the ceiling as the mechanized vibrations from above shook the earth. What they likely did not notice were the accumulating hairline fractures in the limestone strata, the product of many days of dynamite blasting and earthmoving.

This first visit was cut short because the boys had to get home for supper, but they agreed to explore the cave again the following day after school. As they climbed out of the cave system onto the dusty, noisy roadbed, the boys' jubilant mood was cut short by a highway worker warning them away from the work zone. "This is a dangerous place for you kids," he yelled. The boys were told the heavy earthmoving equipment was constantly moving, shaking the ground and kicking up dust, reducing visibility. "Go home! You could get hurt!"

Still, the exuberant boys' hunger for adventure persisted. On Tuesday, May 9, they returned, again darting across the roadbed and entering another gaping cave opening. After exploring for a few hours, they emerged from their subterranean hangout and headed home, their clothes and shoes caked with mud from the roadbed left messy by rain.

The Hoag parents, Mike and Helen, were angry when Billy and Joel showed up looking like filthy waifs in muddy clothing and shoes. A Hoag sibling, sixteen-year-old Debbie, remembered the tongue-lashing the boys received from their parents. "They said if you go in those (cave openings) again you're going to get your motor oiled, and that meant they were going to get a paddling. So, the boys had to go and wash their clothes and clean their shoes," Debbie said.

At Hannibal Junior High School, on the city's northwest edge, the school day on May 10 crawled along. After the final bell signaled the end of studies, Joel raced to his locker and stowed his books before boarding the bus for the short ride home. Ever the inquisitive teen, Joel mentally made plans to do *something* outdoors on this spring day.

Craig Dowell joined Joel on the bus, and the two boys chatted during the ride home about their future adventures.

At the Hoag house, Helen Hoag looked out the door and shouted to her fifteen-year-old son, Tim, as he stepped off the high school bus, instructing him to watch Joel and Billy so they would not go exploring the caves again. "Keep an eye on the boys, and don't let them leave the yard," Debbie remembers her saying. The Hoag parents departed for the grocery store, satisfied they'd put an end to the boys' cave explorations.

After school, Joel changed into blue jeans and a white T-shirt and headed out the front door, again reminded by Debbie to stay close to home. Shortly, he caught up with Billy and Craig to play, the three mindful of the warnings to stay away from the caves.

What they could not have known was that their last day of school was also the last day of their lives.

* * *

John Janes attended eighth grade with Joel and Craig at Hannibal Junior High School. Although new to town, John had already explored parts of the other subterranean cave network, Murphy's Cave, located several blocks north of the Highway 79 roadcut construction area.

"It was pretty routine for kids to go in there. We thought we were spelunkers. What teenage boy wouldn't? It was *there*," Janes said, reflecting back on his adolescent curiosity and lust for adventure.

On the bus ride home from school, Janes and his friend Lynn Strube discussed exploring the cave again. "We got home, changed clothes and rode our bikes down to Murphy's. We'd gone into the cave two or three times with flashlights in the past, but not very far, just far enough we were confident we could find our way back out," Janes said.

Janes estimated he and Strube had entered the cave about four o'clock. "The passages were very small, branching this way and that, and we had to crawl on our belly to get through some of them. We could sit up in some areas, but none of the areas in this particular part of the cave were high enough to stand," Janes recalled.

Meanwhile, outside the cave, Wes Leffert came wheeling down Walnut street shortly after four on his beloved green Huffy bike, packed with the *Quincy Herald-Whig* newspapers he delivered daily to southside subscribers.

As Leffert approached Birch street he saw Joel, Billy and Craig standing by the Murphy's Cave entrance. "As I rode up, they stopped me. They were getting ready to go in and asked if I wanted to go with them," Leffert remembers. "I told them I had to deliver newspapers and to be careful because once you're inside the passages went in many directions, and it's pitch black in the cave. I was glad they had a flashlight with them."

After exploring Murphy's Cave for about twenty minutes, Janes and Strube had turned around and reversed their course out of the labyrinth. "As we were coming out of the muddy entrance, we met Craig, Joel and Billy standing outside waiting to come in," Janes said. "They weren't muddy so we knew they hadn't yet been inside. I think they had a flashlight with them, because you didn't get into that cave very far before you lost daylight."

Janes and Strube stopped and chatted with the boys for a few minutes before mounting their bikes and rolling down the sidewalk. "As we left, I looked back and saw them going into the cave. That was the last time we saw them, probably about four thirty," Janes said.

One of the last individuals to see the boys was retired school teacher Louise Kohler who spent most of her career as a dedicated second grade teacher at A.D. Stowell School. Kohler lived near the Hoags and knew the boys well. "Those boys were nice, no trouble with them," she recalled. "I liked them. They were always polite and seemed intelligent. They were only being boys going out and exploring," Kohler added.

Kohler had first seen the boys after school on May 10 as they meandered down the alley behind her house, talking and kicking rocks with their sneakers. She spoke with the boys who told her they were going to the Stowell playground down the block. It appeared they were obeying their parents' directive to avoid the roadcut caves.

Kohler departed shortly for a teachers' meeting across town, but ended up leaving the gathering early because she was feeling ill. "On my way back home, shortly after five, I saw the boys standing high up on the sloping roadcut, looking down at the big earthmovers. I knew it was them because I recognized their clothing from when I'd seen them earlier that day."

The boys, tempted by adventure, had returned to the very spot the Hoag parents had warned them to avoid.

Meanwhile, janitor Thomas Breedlove was finishing up his custodial duties on the second floor of Stowell School. He glanced out over the rooftops and saw the boys standing on the high slope on the east side of the roadcut, where Mrs. Kohler had seen them minutes earlier. He watched them for a moment and then moved along. The time was a quarter past five.

Even at this hour, the roadcut site was a chaotic scene. Large earthmovers were lumbering back and forth, the ground vibrating, the air filling with swirling, choking dust, causing poor visibility. But the audience of three was suddenly no longer watching the activity below.

After a quarter past five on May 10, 1967, Joel Hoag, Billy Hoag and Craig Dowell were never seen again. Once the Hoag boys failed to show up for supper, Helen Hoag notified the Hannibal Police Department.

REPORT TO HANNIBAL, MO., POLICE DEPARTMENT

Case: Boys Missing
Reported Date: 5/10/67
Time: 6:45 p.m.
Investigated by: All
Desk Man: Dindia

About 6:45 p.m. May 10, report came to the station of 3 boys missing. Edwin Craig Dowell, age 14, 634 Union, Bill Hoag age 11 and Joe Hoag age 13, 621 Fulton Ave. Seem there was indications that they intended to go into a cave believe[d] to be Murphy Cave located in the area of Walnut & Birch and another one North of Murphy Cave. At 7:00 p.m. the Mark Twain Rescue Squad was called in and conducted a search of the caves until early hours of the morning. [Update] This search will resume again this morning. As of 9:00 a.m. May 11 there is nothing to report at this time.

Following is a description of the boys reported missing afternoon May 10.

#1 - Edwin Craig Dowell, 14, dob 12-29-52, 5-10, 155 lbs. medium build, light brown curly hair, blue eyes. Wearing light color trousers, no coat or hat, size 10 shoes either wing tip slippers or loafers.

#2 – Joel Wise Hoag, 13, dob 7-25-53, 5-6, 120 lbs., black hair, brown eyes, medium build, wearing possibly a red trimmed white jacket and blue jeans, and old slippers.

#3 – William Francis Hoag, 11, dob 10-4-55, 4-10, 86 lbs., medium build, dark red hair, blue eyes, wearing tan khaki jacket, blue jeans, and lace boots.

Descriptions given by brother of Edwin Dowell when his parents could not be contacted and by the mother of the Hoag boys.

OFFICER(S) <u>Det. Hendrix</u>

Initially, police officers responded quickly and entered Murphy's Cave yelling the boys' names. Soon, the Mark Twain Emergency Squad members came onto the scene. While squad members were experienced at finding lost hunters and dragging the river for dead bodies, they had no expertise in cave rescue. They also lacked the necessary equipment to safely explore subterranean passages. The squad members erected bright searchlights operated by power generators and began widening some cave openings for easier access. Volunteer townspeople also stepped up to help during the early hours of the search.

What most of the volunteers encountered was like nothing they had ever seen before. The cave network was a vast labyrinth of crisscross passages with a layout much like that of a tree; the passages took a form much like the trunk, limbs and branches, random and complex. Search personnel would follow one passage and then come upon two or three other passages branching off in different directions. If they moved into another passage, they would soon be confronted with two, three or four other passages branching off from the one being explored.

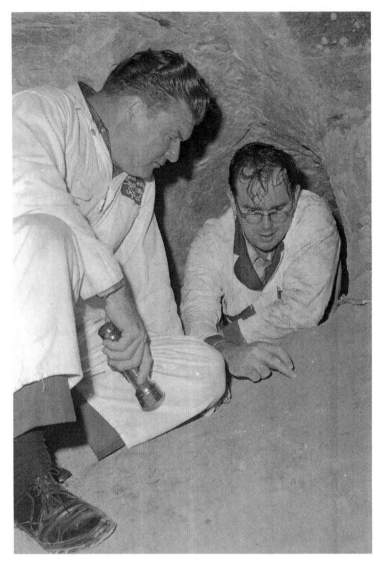

Mark Twain Emergency Squad members inside Murphy's Cave.
Photo courtesy Hannibal Courier-Post.

No matter where they turned in the cave, the environment all looked essentially the same, tannish limestone walls and ceilings and buff-colored silt for a floor. Many of the passages had very low ceilings due to the accumulation of silt over the eons. The search volunteers frequently would have to drop to their hands and knees to traverse a tighter passage. In some areas, the cavers had to lie prone and wiggle like a worm, at times having to exhale so his or her torso could clear an especially tight, coffin-snug portion of a passage.

The volunteers found the cave mostly dry, thanks to a layer of shale above which kept most of the ground moisture out of the cave. The constant temperature of fifty-two degrees foreshadowed trouble. A fall in this unforgiving environment would constitute great misfortune for an injured explorer. Lying still in the cave, injured or trapped, a boy's body heat would be sapped within hours. The search was by necessity slow and complex, as cavers faced nearly two miles of passages within a ten-acre footprint below the rock quarry of my youth.

Neighborhood ladies observe the Murphy's Cave search.
Photo courtesy Dan Bledsoe.

By Thursday morning, law enforcement had issued a call for experienced cavers, and the response was overwhelming. Cavers from Missouri, Illinois, California, and Virginia were soon arriving in Hannibal, ready to begin a search that would last nearly a month. Authorities also had notified William Karras, a Virginia-based cave rescue specialist who had founded the Speleological Society of America (SSA) the previous autumn. The SSA had been established for this type of emergency cave search-and-rescue situation. Thursday night, Karras and his team arrived at Quincy, Illinois' Baldwin Field airport on Air Force II, courtesy of Pentagon brass.

SSA Director Bill Karras with Helen and Mike Hoag during the tense search. UPI photo.

In the following days and weeks, Karras and his team would coordinate a huge caving team as they explored Murphy's Cave, the newly discovered roadcut cave system, and three hundred other cave entrances and grottos across area counties.

In addition, Missouri Governor Warren Hearnes activated 150 members of a Missouri National Guard unit led by Colonel

Bill Tucker, a Hannibal native. The Guard members conducted an extensive above-ground search from Hannibal's southside to Saverton seven miles to the south. They peered into sheds, barns, wells and anything else that could harbor three boys.

A tight passage inside Murphy's Cave bluff. Photo by David Mahon.

The search and rescue operation ran around the clock. Church ladies and women in the neighborhood volunteered to prepare sandwiches, fried chicken, side dishes, beverages and desserts to keep the busy, exhausted cavers fueled for the formidable task underway.

It was a desperate race-against-time search. Karras and the other cavers understood the dynamics; the boys, if trapped in a chilly cave passage, likely had only three days to survive. With no food and water, they would slowly succumb in the fifty-two-degree cave environment. "Once their body temperature hits eighty-eight degrees, they'll go unconscious," Karras darkly informed the team during a late-night meeting. "Another three degrees will be fatal."

The assumption that the boys were underground seemed logical. The trio had been seen exploring the two cave systems the two previous evenings and was last seen near the roadcut cave openings shortly after five. the afternoon of May 10.

There was no indication of foul play at the time, and authorities quickly investigated alleged sightings of the boys by individuals who had seen their photos in the newspaper or on the television newscasts, but none of the leads led anywhere or were simply cases of misidentification.

Mystery Man

Karras and the other team members grew curious when they heard a highway worker mention a *mystery man* who had been seen for two or three days standing on the roadcut slope prior to the boys' disappearance. When a highway worker approached the man and inquired about his presence at the site, the man had simply responded, "I'm just watching the highway construction activity."

Nothing much was made of this man at the time. Later, in Karras' SSA After-Action Report, compiled once the search ended, he referenced the mystery man and noted this individual had given the search parties misleading information about where to search. In his report, Karras did not reveal the nature of this misleading information, unfortunately.

Shortly after the boys went missing, the mystery man, identified as an adult Caucasian, perhaps thirty-five years of age, disappeared and was not seen again as the desperate search continued to unfold.

This stranger set off alarms in the mind of the National Guard's Colonel Tucker. "Riverside Cemetery is nearby, just south of Lovers Leap, so I told my men to check it carefully, especially if there were any fresh graves or signs of recent digging," he explained. "Someone could have killed those boys and dumped them in a fresh grave."

The Highway 79 roadcut search zone. Photo courtesy Steve Chou.

The only item ever found during the ground search was a white sock, a popular brand, discovered in a rock quarry at the Atlas-Portland Cement Plant property a few miles south of the roadcut. It was quickly dismissed as nothing of significance.

After thousands of hours of searching, the cavers grew exhausted, their frayed nerves worn raw by stress and fatigue. Every day they had to face the grieving parents of the Hoag and Dowell boys and tell them there was nothing new to report.

Numerous additional openings were excavated across the east face of the Murphy's Cave hill, enabling cavers to get around passages filled with debris from previous ceiling breakdowns. After nearly a month of around-the-clock activity, Murphy's was more unstable due to exposure to the outside air, the heavy human traffic moving through the cave and extensive digging undertaken in many of the passages.

Cavers outside Murphy's Cave. Photo courtesy *Quincy Herald-Whig*.

At this point, cavers now realized they were risking their own lives as the search had evolved into a body-recovery mode.

Late in the search, Tex Yokum, one of Missouri's top cavers, along with two other cavers, had exited Murphy's Cave when tons of rock collapsed from the ceiling, filling the passage behind them. They had escaped certain death by mere seconds. It was clear, Karras said, the search for human remains was not worth additional lost lives, so the operation was called off.

"The search ended due to its own lack of progress," said caver Joe Tripodi. "After nearly a month and thousands of hours of searching, we'd found nothing and it was pretty clear we were not going to find them. We all went home pretty sad," said the St. Louis caver who spent a month in Hannibal coordinating Rescue Control, the operational nerve center during the search.

In the coming decades, the lost boys' story would again emerge into the headlines. In 1992, the twenty-fifth anniversary of the boys' disappearance, a granite monument honoring the trio was placed on Lovers Leap for future generations to view and ponder the mystery. The families and friends of the boys continue to grieve them. There has been no closure to this terrible story from Hannibal's past. They have spent their lives wondering where the boys' remains lie.

Most of the experienced cavers, who understood the nature of maze caves, suspected the boys were likely killed by a ceiling collapse in the roadcut cave network. After the search, the Missouri Speleological Survey officially named the roadcut system Lost Boys Cave. All entrances to the cave system and those at Murphy's Cave were filled to ensure the dangerous passages remained unavailable to curious explorers. In his after-action report compiled after the Hannibal search, Speleological Society of America President William Karras wrote, "What then, did happen to the boys? My heart cries because we failed to find the boys. It would be better to believe they just went away. I'm at as much a loss why God put this mystery before us as anyone."

Karras' SSA disbanded in 1969, three years after it had been established. He changed his focus from the subterranean world to other endeavors. Always an adventurer, Karras sold snowmobiles in the 1970s and reportedly became the first person to drive a Skidoo brand sled across the United States.

Later, he embraced hot air ballooning in the Pacific Northwest and made it into the record book. On May 31, 1981, Karras and his co-pilot Scott Gardiner attempted the first crossing of the Cascade Mountains by hot air balloon. Taking advantage of good winds, the two men launched from Issaquah, east of Seattle at 12:50 p.m. Four earlier attempts at the ninety-mile crossing by other balloonists had failed.

The men ascended in their massive balloon, the Shenandoah, standing eighty feet high with a girth of sixty-five feet, up to thirteen thousand feet where they found an atmospheric sweet spot, forty-mile-per-hour winds aligned perfectly with their planned flight path. Karras, then fifty-seven, had accrued more than two thousand hours of experience piloting balloons in the previous decade. As captain of the flight, he boldly expressed confidence this fifth attempt would be successful. About five o'clock, the Shenandoah floated over 12,307-foot Mount Adams and began its descent, soon landing seven miles north of the Yakima, Washington airport. The historic, record-setting adventure had taken four hours.

Karras kept his eyes to the heavens, later becoming interested in ultralight aircraft, but this avocation would not last. On May 29, 1983, Karras was piloting an Eipper Quicksilver MX ultralight aircraft near a Memorial Day crowd at a park in Sumner, Washington. Witnesses quoted in the National Transportation Safety Board Aviation Accident Summary said the aircraft had done wing-over maneuvers over the lake and was making a second pass when the engine suddenly cut out. In a moment of alarm, Karras quickly reached over his head to restart the engine. The ultralight aircraft had two fuel tanks, and he noticed the main tank was empty. Karras struggled to open the petcock knob on the other tank to restore fuel flow, but while distracted for these chaotic few seconds the aircraft struck a tree. Karras sustained serious eye and head injuries.

A cave opening in the roadbed of Highway 79.
Photo courtesy *Hannibal Courier-Post*.

Battling bladder cancer, vision troubles and neurological issues, William Karras spent his final years living with his wife Janelle at a senior care facility in Kansas, her childhood home.

I telephoned Karras a few years before his death. The weak, high-pitched voice on the phone revealed a frail and failing man. We spoke briefly, as he acknowledged the frustration everyone felt about the outcome of the 1967 Hannibal search operation.

"It's a real mystery where those boys are. We did our very best to find them. I still think about it." William Gus Karras died on February 22, 2004, his eightieth birthday, at the Halstead Health & Rehab facility in Halstead, Kansas.

Exhausted cavers inside Rescue Control. Photo courtesy Steve Chou.

Tex Yokum, who served as the director for the SSA's Great Plains Region, wrote after the search: "Unless you were an active participant in this massive search, it will be impossible for you to understand the complexities of a project of this size.

Never in the history of caving have cavers engaged in a search as mysterious as this. As far as I know, in every other rescue, operations could be concentrated at one point, since it was known precisely where to look, but not so in this case."

Yokum reported the search had thoroughly targeted a seven-mile radius of Hannibal's city limits, the scope of which had never before been encountered by a cave rescue unit. "My only regret," Yokum wrote, "is that we came away empty-handed. It is extremely distressing when you realize that with all the talent, energy, time, equipment and money expended in this search, we failed to find one single shred of physical evidence concerning the boys." The experienced St. Louis area caver, now deceased, called the historic search a "tremendous test of our ingenuity, stamina, dedication and ability to cooperate."

The former Assistant State Geologist, Jerry Vineyard (now deceased) was involved in cave identification, exploration and preservation for his entire professional life. His belief? "After many days, it became pretty apparent to me that the boys had not run away, and they were not in any other known open caves because we had checked. I think they were under the road and they're still there—if we only knew *where*." Vineyard speculated that the boys could have been in a passage on the western fringe of the roadcut, perhaps even under the Southside Christian Church lawn, and a collapse sealed them away so they couldn't get back out again.

"That roadcut had been drilled and shot (dynamited) and basically was an accident waiting to happen," Vineyard recalled. "They had all this shot rock and openings into it, so I'm convinced the boys went into one of the openings and, while they were in there, the roof fell in on them, and we were just never able to find that spot."

Vineyard visited Hannibal many years after the search and was struck by how normal the area appeared. "The highway department had concreted up the entrances that were on the east side of Highway 79. The area appeared strangely benign compared to having looked very dangerous in 1967 with everything open and raw. Now, vegetation has grown up, and weathering has softened the roadcut features."

Susan DeVier-Baker, a petite caver who helped explore some of the smaller passages in Murphy's Cave and the roadcut system, still contemplates the historic search. She and her husband enjoy the peace and quiet of their 120 rural acres in northern Moniteau County, Missouri. While Susan eventually gave up caving as an avocation, caving has never fully left her. Their property includes Bruce Cave, a popular subterranean destination for scout troops and science clubs from area schools.

Hannibal was her first and last cave search. "After I returned home, the search affected me for quite some time. It was very intense, and there was just no closure. It must have been ungodly for the families to see everyone pack up and just leave town.

"Once in a great while I'll think about it. I gave it my all and did the best I could... we all did. There was just nothing more to be done." Susan says a gut-wrenching thought has never left her: "The worst thing in the world is to not know what happened to a loved one, to know only that they vanished, never to be seen again. That's hard for the families, and it's hard for all of us."

Bob Cowder, a seasoned caver and Missouri National Guard platoon leader who helped with the ground search, quickly grew frustrated by the lack of success during the search. "Nobody really knows what happened, but everyone has a theory," he lamented. "There was just no trace whatsoever of those three young boys. It was just remarkable. That just doesn't happen." Cowder (now deceased) suspected the boys may have met foul play. In an eighteen-month period, he claimed two Quincy women and two individuals from Monroe

City had disappeared. "One of the women was found dead in the river bottoms near Quincy. There just seemed to be a lot of disappearances in the area during that time." It was more fodder, but no concrete leads, to fuel the mystery surrounding Hannibal's missing boys.

Gary Rush, a lifelong Hannibal resident and childhood friend with the lost boys, says his thoughts still turn to the 1967 search. "It's haunting. I would have likely been with them going into the caves on May 10, but I had a guitar lesson that evening. Every time I've read something about the disappearances over these many years, it brings up a lot of emotion because it could have been me too."

Rush believes the boys went into a roadbed opening and were unknowingly buried and trapped. "People came from all over the country to this little town to help us... it was really extraordinary. They say time heals all things, but some things you never really ever get over. When we get to heaven, perhaps we'll know the whole story," Rush said.

The Hoag and Dowell families experienced more pain than most families could ever be expected to bear. After Billy and Joel Hoag went missing, another son, Mikey (Michael Terry Hoag, Jr.), was killed in a February 1968 car accident in Columbia, South Carolina, after a drunk driver hit him head-on.

In October 1975, another Hoag son, Robin, who adored his older brothers Joel and Billy, died in a tragic shooting mishap at age sixteen. "The disappearance of Joey and Billy had taken a toll on him that no one fully realized," said sister Lynnie Hoag-Pedigo. Helen and Michael Hoag's family had lost three sons and brothers in nine months, then a fourth eight years later. It was more pain than any family should have to bear.

Hoag family portrait. Courtesy Lynnie Hoag-Pedigo.

In November 1989, Helen and the kids surrounded Mike Hoag's deathbed. "When he passed," Lynnie explained, "I told Mom, Dad now knows what happened to the boys." Helen nodded agreement, dabbing her eyes with a tissue. Helen, who died in June 1995, once told Lynnie, "God loaned you kids to me, and I don't know for how long." It was a poignant statement from a loving mother who had endured so much emotional pain.

For fifty-one years, many thousands of people in the Midwest and beyond have grieved Joel, Billy and Craig. But during the spring of 2018, a remarkable series of events began to reveal some very different answers regarding this most vexing mystery. And the events would recast the historic narrative in an astonishing way—from missing to murder.

And the scores of cavers who left Hannibal feeling sadness and defeat in 1967 could find comfort, perhaps, in one thing— the boys had not been lost in the cave.

(For the full story of the 1967 cave calamity, read *Lost Boys of Hannibal: Inside America's Largest Cave Search* by John Wingate, Calumet Editions, 2017.)

Chapter 4

"Gacy Did It!"

After the publication of my book *Lost Boys of Hannibal: Inside America's Largest Cave Search* in December 2017, several book signing events were arranged in the Hannibal and Quincy area. Interest in the story remains very strong in the region, and the book's social media has drawn thousands of followers. Countless people remember the event as children or young adults, while others have heard the story from family or friends. As new generations have come along, it seems the interest in this mystery remains as strong as ever.

I assumed the book events would be the completion of a long process that had taken several years as I researched and wrote the book. I would quickly discover this was only a brief respite before the story grew to astonishing proportions and quickly launched me into the next phase of a sad and sordid journey.

The first book signing was held in January at Quincy Books, located at the local mall. An estimated one hundred people were lined up down the corridor, books in hand or ready to purchase a copy at the bookstore. It was as much a reunion as a book signing as I reconnected with many friends from high school and college.

Another similar event was held in March at the Mark Twain Museum in downtown Hannibal. More than 130 people attended this event, making it the best-attended book event in the museum's history. Afterward, given the high interest in the book, we decided to hold another book signing and speaking event at the museum on June 30 for the tourist crowd that visits Hannibal for Independence Day celebrations and activities.

It was a classically hot and muggy summer day in Hannibal when my wife, one of my daughters and I arrived at the end of June. The thermometer hit one hundred degrees by early afternoon, but the extreme sultry weather wasn't the reason this event would prove to be so extraordinarily strange, surreal and memorable.

Mark Twain Museum book event, June 30, 2018. Photo by Annya Wingate.

After being introduced by Henry Sweets, the long-time director of the Mark Twain Boyhood Home and Museum, I took the podium and started speaking about the challenging historical nonfiction book that had taken me several years to research and write. Typically, I speak for thirty or forty minutes and then take questions from the audience.

About ten minutes into my presentation, I noticed a young woman seated in the second row, gazing intently in my direction; her cheeks were flushed red, and tears filled her eyes. She was clearly emotionally overwrought by the sad story of the lost boys, I thought. Appearing to be in her twenties, and too young to have personally lived through the event, I thought perhaps she was the daughter of someone who had known the boys.

I'm always moved by how much empathy there is for the lost boys' story. In a sense, these three boys, Joel, Billy and Craig, were everyone's sons—The Sons of Hannibal—who have never been forgotten despite the passage of time.

Afterward, while signing books, the young woman, Cat Hunt, and her mother approached with their books in hand. Cat was smiling, and the strong emotional response seen earlier had left her eyes reddened. Not wanting to embarrass her, I did not bring up the matter. She shared that as a distant relative of the Hoags, there was always an interest in the story. As a child, she had escorted her mother to the Hannibal newspaper to view news clippings from May 1967. We said our goodbyes, and Cat and her mother departed. The book event again proved to be a success, and we returned home to Minneapolis.

Two weeks later, I received a late-night text message from Lynnie Hoag-Pedigo, the older sister of Joel and Billy, who was eighteen when they disappeared. She urged me to call her, which I did the following morning. When she heard my voice on the phone, a torrent of words came flooding out.

"John! Gacy did it! They were his first kills! At your book event, Cat saw the three boys next to you!"

I couldn't believe what I was hearing. Serial killer John Wayne Gacy from Chicago? I remembered the story as a reporter and news anchor in Peoria, Illinois, during the late 1970s. I refreshed Lynnie's memory. "He was convicted in 1978 for torturing and murdering thirty-three young men and boys and was later put to death in the early 1990s," I related.

"Cat *saw* the boys' spirits at my book signing? Astonishing!"

Lynnie continued rapid-fire. "In the last month, two other psychics have revealed they also channeled the boys and saw Gacy as the killer."

"This is hard to believe," I told her. What on earth, or perhaps beyond this earth, was happening?

As I investigated further in the following months, I discovered three women, two in Missouri and the third in Wyoming, with remarkable abilities as intuitive mediums. Incredibly, these three clairvoyants had supernaturally sensed the same scenario—the abduction of the three boys by John Wayne Gacy and their tortures and murders the very evening they vanished in May 1967.

My mind was swimming. I've never given much thought to psychics; in fact, we know the Bible warns believers to steer clear of anything to do with this unknown realm beyond our physical world. This paranormal stuff is impossible for people to *fully* understand, and there may be the presence of demonic activity that can deceive and even gain a foothold in one's life bringing confusion and torment, as we discovered in Stephen's situation related earlier.

Still, having heard what Lynnie had to say, I wondered if it was possible this new development could be a "God thing." I again recalled Mary Riley's favorite scripture Romans 8:28: *And we know that in all things God works for the good of those who love him, who have been called according to his purpose.*

Had all of the focus and interest about my book, by many thousands of people, catalyzed into an amazing supernatural crusade of hope, something more incredible than science fiction? I had to know more.

* * *

Cat Hunt, twenty-seven, lives in southern Missouri where she works in the financial services industry. Cat Hunt is an assumed name for purposes of this book because, understanding the range of public opinion about psychics and the paranormal, she was worried that using her real name might jeopardize her professional job security. "I want to help, but since I never plan to make a living with my intuitive gifts, I need to remain low profile," Cat explained.

During a summer phone call, Cat told me she first connected with her clairvoyance ability at a young age. "I've been psychic my whole life. I've been seeing things since I was six years old, but it used to scare me so I would just block it. It was during April of 2018 that I really started learning and accepting the gift that I have," Cat told me.

"I see energy really well, so I see energy around the earth and other people. Spirit-wise, my grandfather died when I was two, and we were really close, and I see him from time to time. He used to stand in my room and watch over me at night like my guardian angel. When I was seven, I described to my grandmother my great, great, great grandmother, someone I had never seen."

Perhaps Cat's remarkable gift is genetic, the gift of a special biochemical presence in her DNA that enables her to live in this world and experience the one beyond. Her mother, Carol, also has psychic abilities, periodically sensing premonitions of events still to come. Shy and soft-spoken, Carol shared her story with me during an evening phone conversation as I learned about her paranormal gifts.

"I've always sensed things will happen and then they do, indeed, happen," Carol explained. I asked her to cite an example to help me better understand. One morning, Carol said, she had a vision of answering a ringing phone. A voice on the other end said to her, "This is Cobb County General Hospital in Atlanta." Then, the vision ended as suddenly as it had emerged into her mind and visual field.

The vision shook Carol because it seemed so real, but this paranormal mystery would only continue to mystify and perplex her. Over an eighteen-month period, Carol had this identical wakeful vision six separate times. "I'd be watching TV or reading a book, and all of a sudden I'd get this vision," Carol explained. "Every time it was the same message—'This is Cobb County General Hospital in Atlanta.'"

Finally, she was able to better understand this unusual experience. It was a few hours after midnight on a stormy morning in the early 1990s when the telephone rang for real. When Carol sleepily answered, it was déjà vu all over again. But this time the call was sadly all too real. The caller was a nurse from Cobb County General Hospital in Atlanta relaying some terrible, heartbreaking news. "She told me our son-in-law had been killed in a car accident."

Clairvoyance is Common

While precognitive incidents like Carol's are unusual, they occur more frequently than we might imagine. Dr. Julia Mossbridge, a researcher at the Institute of Noetic Sciences in Petaluma, California, studies this subject matter. For centuries, philosophers as far back as Plato have used the term *noetic* for precognitive experiences that psychologist William Janes described in 1902 as: "...states of insight into depths of truth unplumbed by the discursive intellect. They are illuminations, revelations, full of significance and importance, all inarticulate though they remain; and as a rule, they carry with them a curious sense of authority."

Mossbridge has written about her own close-call story that saved her family from injury or death, thanks to advance prompting. In 2012, she was living with her teenage son and her seriously ill partner who required bottled oxygen for his lung disease.

"One evening I became overly preoccupied with checking that my son had locked his bike away in the garage. I was so concerned I began to yell at him which was totally out of character for me," she said.

Urgently motivated by this obsession, Mossbridge impatiently marched out to the backyard garage where she found the door locked with the bike secure inside. Relieved, she turned to return to the house only to notice the electrical meter was on fire. There was no smoke yet, so she had thankfully discovered the blaze early. It was one of those memorable life moments because her partner's highly flammable oxygen supply was located on the other side of the wall, directly opposite the burning electrical meter.

Mossbridge's unrelenting urge to check the garage door averted what could have been a massive explosion, possibly killing them all. "It was as if the future had reached out, gently pulled me forward and given me a glimpse of what needed to be done," she said, still amazed by the event.

Earlier, at Northwestern University in Evanston, Illinois, while pursuing a Doctorate degree in psychology, Mossbridge had led a team that reviewed twenty-six experiments published over the previous three decades, all of which claimed that human physiology can predict future emotional or important events. She views these precognitive moments, like Carol experienced involving a family death, as pre-warnings that can prepare people for what is coming.

"Precognition can improve people's lives. Precognitive dreams are the most commonly reported psychic experience," she said. "Research suggests 15 to 30 percent of people have experienced this phenomenon."

While Carol's event came months after her first premonition, Mossbridge says these precognitions typically happen about 40 percent of the time on the day after the dream or vision has been experienced.

There is abundant biblical evidence for prophetic visions across history and even today. The prophet Isaiah described the birth of the Messiah Jesus in Bethlehem seven hundred years before the historic moment. The apostle John, in the book of Revelation, was shown intense and detailed visions of future times. These are but two examples; many more are detailed by the major and minor prophets in the Bible. These are Divine works of God and the Holy Spirit, biblical scholars and believers agree.

University of California-Irvine statistics professor Jessica Utts, a former president of the American Statistical Association, worked with Mossbridge on the noetic study. She says the evidence is clear: "Precognition, in which the answer is known to no one until a future time, appears to work quite well."

As always, it is impossible for us to fully understand this phenomenon at present.

Spirits Manifest in Hannibal

These days, Carol rarely uses her psychic gift, but her daughter Cat has grown more comfortable with her abilities over the years to see past and future. "I've done readings for co-workers who have lost family members. It's mostly been family and friends at this point because I am still learning," Cat explained.

As distant relatives of the Hoag family, Cat and Carol have more than a passing interest in the lost boys' story. Like so many, they grieved the loss of these children who died too soon. "My mother and I have been researching the boys for years," Cat explained. "I remember in elementary school going to the Hannibal newspaper and copying the old news clippings from microfilm. When I think about it, I've been researching the boys and thinking about them for the last fifteen years of my life."

But Cat never utilized her budding psychic abilities to try to learn more about the incident, because she felt any attempt would be too confusing and impossible to validate as authentic. "I've never tried to connect with the boys and solve that case because, at this point, I'm too close to the incident. I've read all the stories and heard the theories... are they in a cave, under the highway, in a boxcar? So, I can't make a connection that I can validate because I know too much about their disappearance." Cat explained further, emphasizing the importance of knowing very little about a case before she channels someone or an event. "You have to be distanced enough from the situation so you don't know what you're going to sense. If you know too much, it harms the reading because you can color it with your own knowledge or memories," she added.

Then, Cat related the astonishing news, describing what happened at my book signing event she and Carol attended on June 30, 2018. "When you were standing at the podium talking about the boys, I suddenly saw three energetic orbs to the right of you. I couldn't see them clearly at first because they were bouncing around a lot, but they soon took a hazier [translucent] human form, and I could see they were children. I could tell by their voices."

Astounded, I struggled to wrap my mind around the vision Cat had just revealed. "Their spirits were there? How could this possibly be true?" I asked. "How does this work?"

Cat paused for a moment and then began my education in matters paranormal. "When you connect with spirit it's energy, energetic vibrations, and energy never dies," Cat said. "It just changes form. Spirits are at a higher vibrational frequency than living people, and that's why you can't always see them. What psychics can do is *raise* the frequency or vibration of our bodies higher so we can see and interact with them, or the spirits can *lower* their frequency to be visible to us in our place and time," Cat revealed. "And when my energetic vibration increases it makes me emotional and euphoric, so that's why I was crying at your event because they were right there in front of me."

Cat's tearful presence in the audience at the June book event suddenly made sense.

Soon, the boys' etheric images became clearer, and a supernatural connection was established with Cat. "I tried to ignore them as much as possible, but I didn't do a very good job because they noticed me," she said. "One of them moved closer, stopped and looked right at me and said, 'I think she can see us!' Then, they appeared to my left side, and one of the boys spoke into my left ear, 'Can you see me?' They were trying to talk to me, but I blocked it out. In that situation, I would have been talking out loud while you were speaking, there's a room full of people, and I didn't want to look like a crazy person," Cat said with a laugh. "I thought it was pretty cool, but it's also a bit overwhelming when you're sitting in a quiet, crowded room surrounded by other people," she added.

Cat claims the boys' spiritual energy lingered for several minutes. "You were standing and talking, and they were off to the right, up front with you," she said with certainty.

Cat's mother, Carol, validated the event. She did not see the spirits as Cat had reported but described feeling a chill while sitting next to her daughter at the book event. "That sometimes happens. It's a sensation that you get, so I knew something supernatural was definitely happening at that moment," Carol said.

Seeing Beyond

While mediums often experience paranormal communications a bit differently, most of these intuitive individuals are able to see apparitions, the visible presence of spirits in our world or the realm beyond. Pennsylvania psychic Amanda Linette Meder explained it this way:

> [The deceased] appear to me, exactly like living people, only without physical bodies. They are translucent in color, sometimes appearing in a whitish wispy hue, or other times, appearing in color, just see-through or translucent. Since there is no density of the physical body, they are pulling all of their energy together to appear in person, as they appeared when they were alive. Most of the time, I see them with my physical eyes and the translucence varies. In some cases, they are 95 percent translucent, barely visible, and you have to try hard to see them. Other times, they're only 5 percent translucent, looking very dense and barely see-through at all.

In Meder's experience, she sees the apparitions as translucent forms, as denser air moving across a room, or as a shadow form or flash of light. "And there are many times I do not see them with my physical eyes. I will often close my eyes and see them in spirit, in my 'mind's eye,' similar to the way you would mentally recollect a memory or use your imagination to envision something."

Meder explained it is not easy labor for a spirit to manifest in our world. "It takes a lot of skill and energy to appear as a human in physical form without a physical body to work with." Since Meder has a physical body and can draw upon food, water and heat, she says she will share energy with spirits so they can show themselves and deliver messages, with less work and strain on their part. "This is very draining for me, and during a session I can become very warm and thirsty," she said.

Group Intention

What could possibly be the explanation for Cat's extraordinary apparition experience from beyond in this nearly full museum auditorium? What were the circumstances or elements that came together to create this extraordinary incident on a hot June afternoon?

Cat believes that all of the people in the audience, feeling love and empathy for the lost boys—spiritually united with one heart and one mind on their sad disappearance—attracted the boys' supernatural energy forms. "Typically, in a big gathering of people, with so much energy focused on one thing, the spirits are attracted and will show up," Cat said matter-of-factly.

I pondered the significance of her statement for a moment. It is such a paradox of the human heart, this dual capacity both for altruistic, humanitarian love and immense despair surrounding painful events like the boys' disappearance.

I soon discovered there is an area of human psychology called *Group Intentionality* that studies the impact of a group of individuals focused on a person(s), a circumstance or event. Researchers are discovering that when a group comes together it creates its own energetic resonance arising from the hearts of many individuals, and this appears to sometimes impact reality.

Parenthetically, the Holy Bible speaks of this in scripture; believers are encouraged to pray together and to agree on an uttered prayer. This approach enables the praying individuals to come into a fuller presence with God. Doing so further energizes the prayer and gives power to the human petition before God. In other words, there is power in a group, in essence, a sacred circle that can magnify the effect for a fuller, richer experience.

In Matthew 18:20 it states, *For where two or three are gathered in my name, there I am among them.* If Jesus is in the midst of believers who are praying in agreement, unison and in harmony, that means Jesus is hearing their prayer clearly. God hears all prayers, but imagine the impact when many faithful, passionate and sincere believers pray in unity at the same time.

Pastor Tommy Barnett, PhD, who serves the First Assembly of God Church in Phoenix, Arizona, agrees. "The presence of God in the midst of a church is directly proportional to the amount of prayer that takes place there." Clearly, churches that pray together see the amazing power of God at work, going beyond what *they* can do to what God wants to do *through* believers.

"When a handful of people pray together, Jesus will attend every time. And the Father will not deny the requests of a prayer meeting where Christ is also praying," wrote Megan Hill, author of *Praying Together* (Crossway 2016). "Our prayer meetings have the power of Christ's presence and of His intercession so that anything that pleases Christ, anything that fulfills his purpose, anything that glorifies him, anything he commands or promises or loves, we ask with one voice together with Christ in confident expectation that the Father will answer."

Think of it this way, as stated by Debbie Przybylski of International House of Prayer in Kansas City, Missouri. "When an orchestra is tuning up, everything can sound like a lot of noise. Every instrument is doing its own thing, but when the conductor raises his baton, the instruments come together in harmony and unity. That's how prayer should be when Jesus is the conductor of the gathering."

The clairvoyant mediums interviewed for this book say they see group intentionality manifest frequently, and what happened at my Hannibal book signing is but one of many examples, they say.

While Cat witnessed the three boys' energetic apparitions, she says Gacy did not make an appearance at the book event. But, when she sees a photo of the madman, she gets an instantaneous bad feeling, even though she was born long after his arrest and knew little of his background. "The sight of him makes me nauseous. He is absolutely vile. I feel a lot of negative energy from him."

Soon, the serial killer would make his own appearance in this remarkable story.

The book event experience was so extraordinary, perhaps God had ordained Cat as one of the psychic sleuths to solve the Hannibal mystery. Cat believes so. She recognized the importance of what was happening and felt a deep obligation to help untangle this supernatural mystery and convey the boys' message to those who care and still grieve them.

According to Cat, the boys are seeking final resolution of this case so they can fully be at peace. "The boys want to be heard... they want to be found and put to rest," Cat explained, carefully picking her words. "They want closure like everyone else. That's why I contacted Mary Riley. She's a couple of years ahead of me and has more experience in cases like this. I have never worked on missing persons cases, and this is far beyond my experience, and I'm too close to it all."

Incredibly, it was as if this strange journey already had been fated. Mary Riley's mentor in South Dakota had told her several months earlier that she was going to do something great that nobody else could accomplish, and she would do it with assistance from a relative.

Soon, the phone would be ringing at a ranch in rural Wyoming.

Chapter 5
Paranormal Mayhem in the Night

In southern Missouri, Cat Hunt was struggling to understand the full significance of what she'd encountered at my June book signing event at the Mark Twain Museum. She was only weeks away from beginning a series of classes to become certified as a medium, so she didn't feel fully equipped to pursue any channeling on her own about this important and historic lost boys' incident.

Cat reached out to Mary Riley in rural Wyoming; Mary's husband is distantly related to Cat's spouse. The two women had met once at a wedding, and Cat knew Mary had a solid track record as a psychic sleuth. "I felt Mary was the right medium for this assignment," Cat explained.

Mary quickly agreed to channel the missing boys, an historic mystery that had left thousands of people with no emotional closure for half a century. Mary had not heard of my book, *Lost Boys of Hannibal*, but she recalled an evening years earlier when she and her husband, Tanner, watched an episode of *America's Most Wanted* hosted by John Walsh.

"At the end of the program, they showed a photo of the three Hannibal boys and related the story of their disappearance and how this remains an open case," Mary said. "I just started tearing up, and I turned to my husband and said, 'Oh my gosh, I think I know what happened to those boys. They're never going to find them.' And my husband said, 'Well, how do you know that?' I said, 'Because John Wayne Gacy killed them.'"

At this point, Tanner was unaware of Mary's psychic ability, something she had kept a very low profile, even from her family.

"After watching the show, that has always stuck with me. It was the first time John Wayne Gacy and the boys ever came up for me," Mary added. It would prove to be a prescient moment in the saga of this mystery.

Clairvoyant Mary Riley.

Late on the evening of July 13, 2018, after Mary had put the kids to bed, she settled into a patio recliner on the deck. The sun was setting as she prayed to God for protection and guidance. She was ready to channel Cat's request. As Mary describes the moment, she closed her eyes and relaxed, letting her supernatural process unfold. "Cat had sent me a photo of the boys, and I connected right away and quickly knew what was going on," Mary explained.

Immediately, the humble mother of three was rocked by a sudden sensory wave of imagery and emotion that shook her very being. "I picked up on John Wayne Gacy first. When I channeled him, he said, 'Of course I did it, and they'll never find them.' It made me sick. He seemed ignorant and cocky, utterly remorseless," Mary recalls.

Mary then shared a bombshell with me, explaining that Gacy showed her "He was in Hannibal watching the boys for a couple of days prior to their abduction. He also had his eye on a young highway construction worker."

Mary had not read my book about the lost boys' incident, nor did she know anything about Gacy and his killing spree a generation before she was born. Yet, Mary's vision aligns with the historical facts in the lost boys' case. Recall that highway construction workers had seen a "mystery man" standing high on the roadcut slope for two or three days prior to May 10, 1967. When approached and asked what he was doing, the man only stated that he was watching the construction activity. Colonel Bill Tucker, who led the National Guard ground search by 150 National Guardsmen after the boys' disappearance, said he understood the man appeared to be about thirty-five years old. Gacy, who was twenty-five in 1967, was stocky and looked older than his chronological age. Shortly after the boys went missing from Hannibal's southside, the mystery man was never seen again at the roadcut location.

John Wayne Gacy was Hannibal's mystery man, according to Mary.

"The boys got in his car willingly, and everything was okay initially," Mary continued. "They weren't frightened at

69

this point. They were going to drive somewhere together," Mary said, speaking slowly as she reviewed her notes from the reading.

The Hoag boys were accustomed to hitchhiking and accepting rides from strangers, something their parents and siblings had warned them about many times. But getting a ride from Gacy made sense on May 10; Craig Dowell had to return home because the church bus would be picking him up at six o'clock for the Wednesday evening church youth gathering across town.

"I see Gacy is driving along by some trees, and the boys get nervous, pointing out that he's going the wrong way. But Gacy tells them not to worry, he's taking a shortcut." As Gacy drives, Mary sees the oldest boy, Craig Dowell, sitting in the front passenger seat. The two Hoag brothers are sitting in the back, Joel right behind Gacy and Billy sitting in the rear passenger position. "How do you know the Hoag boys were in the back seat?" I ask. Mary explains that she feels there is a familial love connection between the two of them. "It's clear they are brothers."

Suddenly, Mary sees Gacy "pull out a white cloth from behind him and quickly put it over Craig Dowell's face." The boy struggles briefly against the force of Gacy's powerful forearm and hand, feeling light-headed and confused, then slips into unconsciousness. The cloth, apparently soaked with the sedating anesthetic chloroform, was all part of Gacy's modus operandi.

* * *

We briefly fast forward to the early morning hours of March 22, 1978. Carpenter Jeffrey D. Rignall, twenty-six, was walking on Chicago's near north side, with its many bars and discos, when Gacy pulled up in a late model black Oldsmobile. Gacy leaned out the window and complimented the young man on his tan, acquired during a recent Florida visit, and offered him a ride and some marijuana. Rignall got in the car, grateful for the lift on a terribly cold night with wind chills well below zero.

Moments later, before they were halfway through the joint, Gacy pulled out a rag soaked with chloroform and forcefully held it over the young man's nose and mouth. Rignall became disoriented and lost consciousness. Minutes later, he roused briefly in a daze to see a blur of passing street signs outside the car window. Gacy again covered his face with the chloroform rag, and the young man again slumped back into unconsciousness. Rignall awakened later to find himself in Gacy's house with a stunning scene playing out before his glassy, unbelieving eyes. Rignall had been fastened to a wooden rack with holes cut for his head and arms. The wooden contraption, suspended by chains, would keep him immobilized during the imminent sexual assault. Equally disturbing, Gacy stood buck naked before him, and spread out on the floor were several sex toys that Gacy remarked would be used to sadistically rape and torture his unwilling prisoner. Then, the chloroform-soaked rag was again used to send the victim plunging back into darkness.

When Rignall regained consciousness, a few hours had passed, and he was lying at the base of a statue in Lincoln Park. He did a quick self-assessment and found he was suffering from facial irritation and rectal bleeding. He stumbled back to his girlfriend's house, and she drove him to Northwestern Memorial Hospital where he remained for six days. Rignall reported the incident, but police were skeptical of the story.

Not one to let this horrific assault pass, the enterprising Rignall later set up his own surveillance in the area for three days and finally spotted his attacker's car. Rignall scribbled down the license plate number and called the police who traced the car to Gacy. The depraved assailant, still months away from having his killing spree discovered, was charged with battery. By the time the courts could consider the Rignall case, Gacy had already been arrested on murder charges, and the case fell by the wayside. Despite his assault, Rignall, now deceased, was fortunate. Few young men had walked away after an evening with Gacy. Why was Rignall one of the fortunate few to survive? This may be due to the fact that Rignall had sensed the presence of another person at Gacy's place the night of the assault.

Later, another Chicago man hitched a ride with Gacy, and he too had a chloroform-soaked rag forced over his face. He fought off Gacy, opened the car door and fled into the night, another of the lucky ones.

Gacy was consistent with his methods.

* * *

With the Dowell boy disabled in the front seat of Gacy's car, Mary says the Hoag brothers become very "freaked out" in the back seat because they now realize the innocent offer of a ride has gone terribly wrong. The boys slide over to the rear passenger door, four arms flailing and reaching for the door handle, but the door is either locked or jammed, Mary explains. Gacy has quickly pulled the car over and opens the rear driver's side door. The boys slide back across the seat to try to get out this door, but Gacy stops them.

Using a club that Mary says resembles a small baseball bat, the madman knocks Joel unconscious, sending him slumping to the ground. "The other Hoag boy, who is also hit, shows me his airway was blocked like Gacy was choking him. 'It makes my throat hurt, and it's hard to breathe,'" Mary reveals.

She explains that Gacy took both Hoag boys and put their bodies in the large trunk of the car, which she believes was a bluish or green color. "I get a quick glimpse of what looks like a Chevy emblem, and the car's trunk is huge." Efforts to identify the make and model of the car Gacy was driving in 1967 were unsuccessful. Spokespersons for the Iowa and Illinois motor vehicle registration agencies told me records for this time period no longer exist.

Mary says John Wayne Gacy resumes driving. "When Craig Dowell starts coming to, Gacy puts the rag over his face again and again and then slams Craig's head into the passenger window, and he goes unconscious again."

While Gacy is driving, Mary inexplicably sees a set of four numbers that mystify her: 45-33-3-9. I'll explore the possible significance of these numbers later.

Mary next sees Gacy driving on a narrow dirt lane with two rutted tire tracks that lead into a heavily wooded area, well hidden from the paved road they'd previously driven. "He turns the engine off, takes the Dowell boy out of the vehicle and sodomizes him with a club resembling a small baseball bat or a wooden handle of some kind," she said, adding that the vision sickens her.

Mary continues, "To the left of the car, I see a grave that I feel was dug before they got there. It's not deep, maybe three or four feet." Mary says she's headachy, her breathing grows labored and her chest is heavy, sensing that Gacy had strangled Craig Dowell, again the typical killing method the serial killer would use years later in Chicago.

Mary sees the killer dragging Dowell's lifeless body into the open grave. Gacy's killer personality has taken over. Gacy, now well into a full demonic killing rage, turns and walks with an evil single-mindedness to the back of the car. Throwing open the trunk, he pulls out Joel Hoag and drops him to the ground. Mary sees Gacy sodomizing the older Hoag boy, then strangling him too. Joel is the second victim this night to go into the open grave.

"The last boy [Billy] wasn't sexually abused," Mary explains. "I feel like Gacy was starting to get worried. He makes me feel like he was really uneasy and rushed for time and had, perhaps, taken on more than he could handle." Mary sees Billy being hit repeatedly and then rolled into the grave with his brother and friend.

Then, the evil of this day was suddenly over; Gacy's depraved and wicked compulsion had been satisfied at a terrible human cost. Mary senses the sun had set by the time the grave was filled. It would have been sometime after a quarter past eight when the killer departed the wooded area.

In Hannibal, just a few miles to the north, the Mark Twain Emergency Squad was beginning to search Murphy's Cave and the roadcut cave system where the three boys had been seen hours earlier.

During the channeling session, Mary had visions of several items: a red pocket knife that was taken from one of the Hoag boys, a red and gold plaid shirt, a white T-shirt, brown lace-up ankle boots, the bottom of a white sneaker and a silver men's watch with a stretchy band. We know that Joel Hoag had changed into a white T-shirt after getting home from school on May 10, and he often carried a pocketknife.

Gacy's First Kills?

After the astonishing glimpse into the unknown realm, Mary was reeling with emotion as her own three children lay in their beds safe and asleep. "I had to go and be alone and cry for a while. It was very hard, just overwhelming," she says, her eyes brimming with tears. "I've channeled suicides, car accidents, and missing people before and seen graphic things, but this is well beyond that."

Then Mary makes a striking statement that rewrites history. "I feel like these were Gacy's first murders or among his very first. There was just no remorse, no feeling. I just felt a cold, dark energy that was exhausting. It was hard to sleep that night as I lay awake wondering how a human being could do that."

Mary's visions have completely rewritten the ending of the lost boys' mystery and, if correct, revealed that Gacy was wielding his atavistic violence well before he dispatched his thirty-three Chicago area victims between 1972 and 1978.

It was a remarkable, unforgettable evening on this July Friday the thirteenth.

Now, let's review those numbers Mary recalled from her initial channeling session. While Gacy was driving with the boys in the car, Mary saw the numbers 45-33-3-9. What could they represent? I pondered and prayed about this for several days. Were they distances or names of county roads? Then, I realized, perhaps, the numbers told a story that revealed the scope of John Wayne Gacy's evil depravity.

> 45: After his arrest, Gacy told a Des Plaines Police Department officer that he believed the number of his victims was closer to forty-five.
>
> 33: The number of Gacy's Chicago area victims tortured and killed during the 1970s.
>
> 3: The number of boys killed in the Hannibal area, assuming the psychics are correct.

That would make for a total of thirty-six known victims. Subtract thirty-six from forty-five, and you have the final number nine. Could nine be the number of additional Gacy victims that remain unknown and undiscovered? After growing up in Chicago, Gacy also lived in: Las Vegas, Nevada; Springfield, Illinois; Waterloo, Iowa; and then back to Chicago. And he was a frequent traveler. Had he killed additional boys in other cities? I'll explore this later in the book.

Mary's psychic revelations gave all of us plenty to ponder in the coming week. Here we had the abduction of three boys, their torture and murders all laid out like a Hollywood storyboard as revealed by this quiet and kind young mother. It was almost too difficult to fathom.

A few days later, Mary revealed her findings to some of the Hoag boys' surviving siblings, explaining to their great relief that the boys were at peace with their parents. "Of course, I believed it," Lynnie Hoag-Pedigo said. "Yes, I was sad and hurt, but at least I know they are at peace. Maybe we can have some closure finally, *knowing* what happened and *knowing* they're with Mom and Dad. If everything the psychics saw is correct, the boys are close to home."

"I just got sick to my stomach, it upset me so bad. But this is what happened, I just know it is," said Denise Hoag-Mudd who was five in 1967. "It gives me hope though. If they can see all this, maybe they could know where the boy's bodies are located. Maybe they can hit on the spot so we can find them." It was encouraging news for loved ones who knew all too well the feelings of despair and hopelessness. Suddenly, they had a preternatural lead in the lost boys' case.

This was the strangest story I had ever encountered, literally an out-of-this-world experience. It brought me closer to my faith as I prayed daily both for God's protection and His guidance as I struggled to make sense of this information from beyond our present reality, a non-physical place of frequency and energy beyond space-time. There, on the other side in this unknowable realm, beyond space-time, the events of May 1967 happened only an instant ago. According to these psychics, the energetic fingerprints of this calamity remain, waiting to finally be perceived and interpreted by mediums with the proper sensitivity.

I wondered what else the future held for this bizarre story. Then, in late July, a sign. It was a normal morning in the Riley household. Mary was giving the baby a bath, and her iPad was sitting on the dresser in the adjacent bedroom.

"I suddenly heard voices talking so I looked into the bedroom and saw the iPad was playing a YouTube video about the three lost boys in Hannibal. I started to freak out because I didn't want to know anything about the incident while I was involved with the case, so I hurried over and shut it off." Mary says about the same time this happened, their television and other electronics were acting oddly too. Somehow, Mary claims, the iPad browser had called up the video and played it without a human hand touching the device. Could the iPad video have been found earlier by her husband or one of the children?

"Tanner doesn't use this iPad... it's the home school tablet that the kids play games on. We never let them get on YouTube because of the strange things you can see. It's not used for that, only for school activities," Mary explained.

The Riley's were accustomed to paranormal things happening in their former home in South Dakota; lights would go out, objects would move, car keys would disappear only to appear elsewhere. Once, a brass figurine on the piano flew into the air at Tanner who quickly reached his hand out to catch it before being struck in the chest.

But here at the Wyoming ranch, all had been quiet with no paranormal activity. So, what did she make of the iPad incident? "I think it was just spirit saying, *hey we're here, don't give up*. Spirit will give you signs and sometimes it's weird signs like that."

With the extraordinary Hannibal event now evaluated by two of the three psychic mediums, the investigation moved on to the next medium, a young mother named Britney Buckwalter. Her revelations completely unnerved me as this true story grew more incredible. The mystery and wariness I had initially felt delving into these paranormal matters transmuted into full-blown astonishment. Buckle up.

Chapter 6
"John, John, John, John!"

"Britney saw Gacy, and she told me he did it. She saw a cave and then said, 'Oh my goodness, your brothers were among those missing boys.'"

> Denise Hoag-Mudd, sister of Joel and Billy Hoag,
> during a telephone interview with the author.

* * *

Britney Buckwalter was born in May 1988 in Kentucky where her father served in the US Army at Fort Campbell, one of the largest military bases in the world encompassing more than 102,000 acres along the Kentucky-Tennessee border. From her first breath, Britney was special from the other newborns in the base hospital's obstetrics ward, but she would not know why for several years.

Later, the family moved to Palmyra, the county seat of Marion County Missouri, twelve miles from Hannibal and seven miles west of the Mississippi River, locations prominent in the writings of native son Samuel Clemens who wrote under the pen name Mark Twain. Once a hotbed of Civil War skirmishes, Palmyra, with its 3,600 residents, is now a quiet neighbor to historic Hannibal where Britney now lives and works.

Clairvoyant Britney Buckwalter.

Britney, thirty-one, with blonde hair and green eyes, hung out her shingle several years ago when she launched a small business providing intuitive medium and life counseling services for tri-states clients. "I've always been aware I experience things differently from others, and years ago I realized I could help people with my ability."

It was Britney's attendance at a psychic event that changed the direction of her life. "I was picking up on things while I was in the audience at the event." Later, she conducted her own readings with several friends and acquaintances and "I read them with 100 percent accuracy," Britney explained.

Years earlier, Britney was struggling to find a more fulfilling career path. A talented hair stylist, model and pageant competitor at the time, she sensed there was something more for her. As she prayed about her future, she began to see the number four, frequently in the form of 444. "Everywhere I went, I saw 444. I thought it was a sign, but I was also too skeptical to open my mind enough to consider this could be more than coincidence."

Britney discovered that the significance of 444, in the scientific field of numerology, represents Divine messages from on high; clues or guideposts to assist on a journey of awakening on a higher spiritual plane. The takeaway message is to trust the way your life is unfolding, she believes.

It is interesting that the number four has biblical significance too. In Genesis, four is the number of creation, of completeness or wholeness. God completed creation of the universe on day four. Four is the number of elementals in our world: earth, air, fire and water. The regions of the earth total four: north, south, east and west. There are four seasons. There are four gospels that tell the story of Jesus. The fourth commandment directs us to keep God's Sabbath day.

All of this biblical truth and symbology was swimming in Britney's mind for weeks. Then one day, while driving in heavy traffic, Britney found herself stuck behind a slow-moving tractor obliterating her view of the congested highway ahead. As she crept along, all she could see was a spray-painted message on the back of the tractor—444. "And I was forced to sit there and look at it for what seemed like forever," she said, laughing. "So, by the time I got home, I knew I had the support of God and His angels to be myself and settle into this ability and use my gift."

This mother of two small children is energetic with a positive attitude, always staying in touch with clients to see how they are doing, whether it's for a job search, healing from family grief or repairing broken relationships. She has sat with the loved ones of suicide and murder victims to help bring clarity to the painful losses, so loved ones can move beyond the deep grief. "I love all my clients," she says. "Love is what drives the universe. God is love."

Raised as a Lutheran, Britney remains a faithful Christian who believes her intuitive abilities are a true blessing from God. "God created everything. He is the God of the heavens and earth," she proclaims, "and we know that God doesn't make mistakes. So, I don't believe there has to be a separation between belief and faith in God and spirituality." In our world today, that statement illustrates the controversial tug-of-war between biblical truth and New Age beliefs, which I'll explore in chapter nine. I must add that most of what the New Age represents is rejected by the psychics in this book.

Before she conducts a reading, Britney prays quietly for Divine protection and guidance so she can accurately interpret what she senses. "I *always* pray, and I've never experienced anything too scary or dark," she explains. That would soon change as she channeled a most extraordinary event that occurred more than two decades before her Kentucky birth.

Britney acknowledges that most people struggle to understand the mysterious nature of psychic abilities, something so extraordinarily different from daily life here in the earthly plane, but she believes this supernatural gift completely affirms the laws of physics we learned in high school. "We're all made up of atoms and energy, and energy cannot be destroyed, it only changes from one form to another. When we die, our energy leaves the mortal physical body and moves across into the spiritual, non-physical realm, where it exists forever," she says.

It is in heaven where we find the domain of the Triune God/Jesus/Holy Spirit and the Divinely created angels. In the realm of the heavenlies, that etheric realm surrounding our three-dimensional world, there are good spirits and demonic spirits, those former angels cast out of heaven along with Satan after the rebellion as detailed in the Bible. Britney says she has seen angels and believes she clearly understands the difference between sensing good energy versus dark, demonic energy.

All of her human senses are active, Britney explains, when she conducts a reading. She can smell, taste, hear, see and feel vibrational energy from beyond while engaged. "Energy is my first psychic language. It comes as a thought that pops into my mind."

As an example, she relates the story of a missing twenty-one-year-old Hannibal woman, Christina Whittaker, who vanished November 13, 2009. The young woman, who suffered from a bipolar disorder, had enjoyed too many tequila shots at a Hannibal bar and was asked to leave after being unruly with the patrons.

When Britney focused on the missing person case, she saw the Caucasian woman accepting a ride from a black man who drove her to a party on Hannibal's southside. While at the party house, the woman apparently witnessed something she should not have seen, perhaps a drug deal. A man tells her escort to "Get rid of her." Britney then sees Christina's driver and escort sexually assaulting her on a riverbank.

"I can still hear the crunching sound as Christina's hands desperately clawed the dried leaves while she was being sexually assaulted," Britney says, her eyes closed as she recalls the dreadful vision. "Every time I walk on dried leaves and hear that crunching sound it vividly takes me back to that terrible moment."

Officially, the Whittaker case remains open and unsolved at the Hannibal Police Department, but Britney believes Whittaker's body was dumped in the river.

The young psychic maintains most people have this intuitive ability to varying degrees. As an example, she mentions individuals who think of someone shortly before the person calls on the telephone. "I believe just as God has given those born with beautiful voices the ability to sing, He has given others the natural born ability to be more intuitively in touch with spirit and the rest of the world. I can't sing very well, but my intuition is strong. Pure intuition is a God-given ability like any other giftedness," Britney explained.

An Astonishing Reading

On May 4, 2018, Denise Hoag-Mudd, the missing Hoag boys' younger sister who was only five when they vanished, visited Britney and introduced herself as Denise Mudd, not mentioning her maiden name. She took a seat and listened as Britney began the reading. The young psychic quickly connected with Denise's mother, Helen, who died in June 1995. Britney told Denise that her mother is at peace now. She also correctly revealed several personal facts and memories known only to Denise and her deceased mother.

"Anything you'd like to ask her?" Britney gently inquired, as the reading progressed. Denise was quick to respond. "Yes, I want to know where they are." Suddenly it was as if a clap of thunder had echoed across the unknown realm into the room they occupied. "The moment Denise asked the question, I saw the words John Wayne Gacy," Britney says. "His image flashed into my mind. I also saw the three boys walking up a hill. I felt like it was tiring for them to hike up it."

Britney, as a millennial, knew very little about Gacy, knew little about the lost boys' cave search event in 1967, and was unaware of the book I had written about the calamity.

Britney sat back and looked at Denise and said, "They're not in any cave. Without a doubt, I can tell you that it was John Wayne Gacy," Britney told the Hoag sibling. The revelation was upsetting to Denise because she knew that Gacy had tortured his victims before killing them.

The reading continued. Britney senses the three boys went with Gacy thinking they were getting a lift home. "I see this big hill, I see the boys faces, there's a cave nearby and a dusty, grayish blue vehicle. It was late, they were trying to make it home, so they hitched a ride. They thought they were going home, but they weren't," she said darkly. "I clearly see the boys with him."

Had Gacy's car been parked at the base of Lovers Leap bluff near the highway construction zone? The boys were last seen on the steep roadcut slope shortly after five o'clock in the afternoon of May 10, 1967, near the cave openings they had previously explored in the dusty and rocky roadbed. It appeared, according to Britney, that the trio had encountered Gacy near this location and accepted a ride from the persuasive killer.

Suddenly, the reading grew more astonishing as the veil between here and beyond opened wider as Britney directly connected with the Hoag boys' energy. "I said, boys step forward here, and the brothers were saying together, at the exact same time, 'John-Wayne-Gacy. John, John, John, John,' over and over again." Both Britney and Denise were taken aback by the energetic response, both agreeing it was a very unsettling moment. "I got a chill, and that rarely happens," Britney explained.

If what Britney sensed is true, these boys, long deceased, had identified their killer from beyond. These three boys, denied their human potential, their opportunity to grow into men, to have their own families, had done a most remarkable and just act. Five decades after they had been snatched away on a spring evening, they had identified their killer.

Thousands of people have grieved the lost boys these many years, having no closure, no graves to visit. Were we now getting closer to finally knowing what transpired? Would this path reveal the truth? I was compelled to know more, despite the bizarre nature of this story.

Britney revealed the boys had first met Gacy on Monday, May 8, two days before they went missing. He had plenty of time to observe the boys and plan his next moves, while they played in and around the roadcut cave openings.

Britney admitted difficulty connecting with Gacy because she felt an evil, dark energy across the supernatural abyss. "It's very draining and makes me ill. It's hard to do," she acknowledged. "I feel that killing the boys was an escape or release for him. He enjoyed the torture and killings. I just feel sick channeling this," she says, putting a hand to her stomach.

Britney was beginning to develop a fuller sense of the Gacy psyche, a madman overtaken by demons and suffering from a split personality. "Gacy comes across as sly and a smart aleck. He's honestly pure evil. I don't like to stay connected very long because he makes my skin crawl," Britney complains. "He doesn't linger long. He just comes in, shares information, and is gone."

Then, she reveals something totally unexpected. "One more thing—he's seeking redemption." Incredibly, I ponder the irony of her statement. Could John Wayne Gacy really feel remorse and seek redemption for his terrible crimes, even now? Wherever he is in the *non*-heavenly realm, and he must surely be in hell, that hope remains a pipe dream only God could answer. But it's unlikely. Gacy's judgment was set the moment he died—destination hell.

While channeling, Britney also sees the name *Jack* several times. "I scribbled the name six times. I saw it repeatedly," she explains. This is a reference to the other personality Gacy revealed to Cook County authorities in the 1970s. *Jack* was the killer side of his twisted psyche who emerged from time to time to destroy innocent young lives. Jack did the dirty work and chose the method of death Britney now sensed for Joel, Billy and Craig.

"I feel restricted in the throat area," Britney said, raising a hand to her neck. "I feel like he strangled each and every one of them after he had knocked them unconscious first," she added. Tortured and strangled—just as thirty-two of the thirty-three other Gacy victims would be dispatched during the 1970s.

The reading unnerved Denise, who sat there with tears in her eyes as she processed this most terrifying and remarkable news. "I tried to dismiss it," she said. "I don't want it to be real because I don't want to think they went through any suffering. But the reading also gave me some hope that we will get some answers."

After Denise had departed into the bright spring sunshine, Britney gathered herself and made a cup of tea. The reading had left her rattled and shaken, one she'd never forget. "I'm so in shock because I know what happened," she later shared, "and being a part of something that is so big and devastating just shakes my soul."

Chapter 7
John Wayne Gacy

After the Hannibal cave search ended in June of 1967, the pastoral town slowly began its return to normalcy in the wake of the traumatic, calamitous spring. More than a decade had passed until December 21, 1978, when psychopath John Wayne Gacy was arrested in Chicago for the torture and murders of those thirty-three young men and boys.

John Wayne Gacy arrest, December 1978. Photo by *Chicago Tribune*.

Once the Gacy story broke, many people who remembered the 1967 cave search incident wondered whether the Hannibal boys were among the serial killer's victims. It is widely known that the boys had accepted rides from total strangers to get across town or down to Mark Twain Cave, behavior they had been warned about many times. But all of Gacy's known victims were in the Chicago area. What reason would Gacy have for being in Hannibal? I will explore this question in a later chapter. While Hannibal authorities had no evidence of foul play back in 1967, it was a big question that set off intuitive alarm bells in my mind, a worrisome thought that never went away, despite the lack of any real evidence.

Beginning in 1972, Gacy assaulted, tortured and murdered his thirty-three known victims. All of them were slain in his suburban Chicago home after being enticed there by deception or force. Twenty-six of the victims were buried in the crawl space under his modest ranch house in Norwood Park Township. Three other bodies were buried elsewhere on the property, and four victims were dumped in nearby rivers.

Gacy was caught, convicted and served prison time until his death by lethal injection at Illinois' Stateville Correctional Center on May 10, 1994, coincidentally the same month and day the lost boys had gone missing twenty-seven years earlier.

Cook County Sheriff's Department detectives have worked tirelessly over the decades to identify Gacy's victims. As of the publication of this book, only six victims remain unidentified. During the past decades, detectives have quietly taken DNA samples from the surviving relatives of young male missing persons across the US and entered the results into the National Crime Information Center's (NCIC) Combined DNA Index (CODIS), the Federal database operated by the FBI and linked with law enforcement agencies nationwide. In more than two dozen cases, Chicago authorities have matched samples with

DNA from Gacy's victims, enabling law enforcement authorities to finally close many missing person cases and bring closure for the grieving families.

During early 2018, two surviving Hoag sisters submitted their DNA to be included in the Federal database to help with identification of any remains that may be discovered in the future. Coincidentally, the NCIC Federal database first became operational as a crime-solving tool in May 1967 when the boys went missing.

St. Louis area policeman Daniel Hoag, the brother of Mike Hoag, father of Joel and Billy, needed to know the answers to questions that persisted in his mind. After Gacy's arrest, officer Hoag sent the dental records for the three missing Hannibal boys to Cook County Sheriff's investigators, but the dental charts did not match any of the remains that had been recovered in the Chicago area.

Hannibal native Steve Sederwall, who was good friends with Craig Dowell at Hannibal Junior High School, is a retired law enforcement officer who resides in Lincoln County, New Mexico, where he now investigates cold criminal cases, most of them from the nineteenth century. Sederwall discovered some intriguing information from Cook County detectives still working to close the books on Gacy's murder victims' identities.

"Gacy apparently kept meticulous records of his travels. Police know his travels had taken him to the Louisiana, Missouri area and Waterloo, Iowa," Sederwall said. At the time the boys went missing, Gacy and his wife and children lived in Waterloo, Iowa, a four-hour drive from Hannibal. Louisiana is in Pike County, less than thirty miles south of Hannibal. Cook County Sheriff's authorities confirmed they had a gas receipt from the early 1970s that was found in Gacy's belongings after his arrest. The receipt confirms a possible pattern of travel through Missouri previously.

89

You'll recall that psychics Britney Buckwalter and Mary Riley confirmed a suspicion Sederwall and I have long held that Gacy was the mystery man who lingered at the roadcut watching the Highway 79 road construction activities, then vanished shortly after the boys disappeared. As it turns out, Sederwall and Daniel Hoag were both seasoned cops blessed with good instincts and a curious persistence for the truth.

*　*　*

Gacy had come to Waterloo in 1966 after living in Springfield since 1964. Then twenty-two, Gacy managed Robert's Brothers, a men's clothing store in Springfield. While in the capital city he'd met and married Marlynn Myers, a personable young woman from a well-to-do family. Gacy immersed himself in community life, being elected the Jaycee chapter's first vice president and named Man of the Year in 1965. "He was a very bright person, energetic and never displayed any abnormal signs," said Ed McCreight, one of Gacy's Jaycees friends. McCreight said the only unusual behavior he witnessed was when Gacy placed a flashing red light on his car while working a parade route for the Jaycees.

After the move to Waterloo, Gacy helped manage three Kentucky Fried Chicken restaurants owned by Fred Myers, Marlynn's father. It was a heady time for the twenty-four-year-old. Gacy had landed a lucrative job, joined the local Jaycees and helped raise funds for community projects. In 1967, he was named Outstanding Vice President of the Waterloo Jaycees chapter. Jaycee member Charles Hill, a local motel manager at the time, said Gacy was ambitious. "He was a real go-getter. He did a good job and was an excellent Jaycee."

The Gacys bought a three-bedroom, two-bath ranch home at 2716 Fairlane Avenue, a 1012-square-foot starter home built in 1961. Gacy's wife gave birth to a son in early 1966 and a daughter in March of 1967. Gacy was building a family, hoping it would be a happier one than his own.

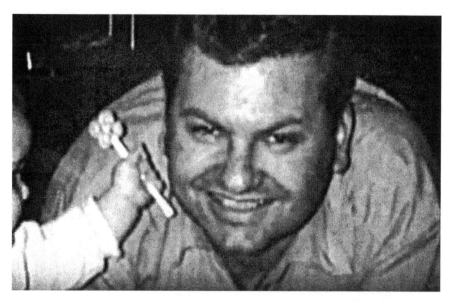

John Wayne Gacy in Waterloo, Iowa in 1967. Provided image.

When Gacy's parents visited the young family in Waterloo, his father, John Stanley Gacy, reportedly apologized for the physical and mental abuse he had inflicted throughout John's childhood. When Gacy was a boy, his stern authoritarian and alcoholic father apparently saw something in young John's personality that was concerning. Feeling a good spanking was beneficial, the father administered the rod regularly. Now, visiting his son in Waterloo, he could only make a curious statement, "Son, I was wrong about you."

While the abuse had ended long ago, the seeds of trauma remained rooted in Gacy's mind. While in Waterloo, Gacy's true nature emerged. He regularly cheated on his wife with prostitutes and operated a teen club in his basement for his young male restaurant employees. Some of the minors were offered alcohol and marijuana before Gacy made sexual advances. When he was rebuffed, Gacy would laugh off the behavior as merely a crude joke.

In March of 1968, the teenage son of a Waterloo Jaycees member told his father Gacy had sexually assaulted him the previous summer. Gacy was indicted on a sodomy charge on May 10, 1968, oddly, *exactly* one year after the boys had gone missing in Hannibal.

By now, public sentiment was turning against Gacy. A fellow Jaycees member said of Gacy after the sodomy charge, "He was not a man tempered by truth. He seemed unaffected when caught in lies."

A court-ordered psychiatric evaluation concluded Gacy had Antisocial Personality Disorder and given his behavioral tendencies was unlikely to benefit from therapy or treatment. The psychiatrist's conclusion? Police had not heard the last of John Wayne Gacy as his behaviors would likely continue to conflict with the norms of a civilized society. It was a prescient warning from a professional who likely understood Gacy's mind better than anyone else at that time.

Gacy was convicted of the sodomy charge and sentenced to ten years at the Anamosa State Penitentiary near Cedar Rapids, Iowa. His wife filed for divorce, and Gacy never saw her and their two children again.

In prison, Gacy was a model prisoner. The prison had rules, and he understood rules. It was life on the outside Gacy struggled to navigate when left to his own instincts. While incarcerated at Anamosa, Gacy helped operate the prison Jaycee chapter, worked in the kitchen and took classes to finally earn his high school diploma. "He had no particular problems during his stay. His adjustment was exceptionally good," according to Warden Calvin Auger who was quoted in the New York Times. "He was a good worker, a willing worker." Auger also reportedly said there was no evidence of homosexual behavior by Gacy while he was incarcerated.

When his abusive father died on Christmas day 1969, Gacy reportedly collapsed and sobbed uncontrollably in his cell. His request for a temporary release to attend his father's funeral in Chicago was denied by the warden. The close bond he so desperately sought with his distant father was never achieved.

In June 1970, Gacy was paroled, and he moved to Chicago to live with his mother. He joined the Democratic Party and got involved in civic activities. Once reestablished in Chicago, Gacy found employment as a cook at a Chicago restaurant. He bought a tan, brick ranch home with his mother and sisters at 8213 West Summerdale Avenue in suburban Norwood Park Township. It didn't take long for the psychopath to fall into his old habits. He was charged with disorderly conduct for forcing a young boy he had picked up at a bus terminal to perform sexual acts on him. But the charge was later dropped when the boy failed to appear in court.

In June of 1974, Gacy married Carole Hoff, a divorcee with two daughters. She was attracted by Gacy's charm and generous nature, but she would soon learn the terrible truth about her betrothed. The couple entertained regularly and became good friends with the neighbors. "He was a kind, friendly and generous neighbor," Lillie Grexa told a reporter years later. "We were close neighbors. Our house was open to him, and his was open to us."

During a visit to the Gacy home, a terrible stench was noticed by the neighbor who suggested, perhaps, a rat had died in the house. Gacy rejected the notion, blaming the odor on moisture in the crawl space beneath the house.

Only Gacy knew the big secret. The crawl space had become a graveyard, the final place of disposition for the young boys Gacy would bring to the house for late night action, later to be drugged, tortured and killed. His first victim, Timothy Jack McCoy, sixteen, died from stab wounds in January 1972, but

Gacy's other Chicago victims were tortured, raped and slowly strangled or asphyxiated. Despite the presence of this sickening odor, Gacy enjoyed throwing frequent, well-attended barbecue parties at his home, thriving on the attention his considerable ego demanded.

Gacy launched a Chicago area contracting business in 1974, PDM Contractors, Inc., hiring teenage boys to handle the painting, decorating and maintenance jobs. Always seemingly surrounded by young boys, his wife suspected her complicated spouse had homosexual desires. She found gay porn magazines around the house and noticed several billfolds in Gacy's dresser drawer. In the garage, where Gacy regularly spent hours late at night, she found a mattress and a red light. When she questioned the killer about these items, he flew into a rage and threw a chair across the room. He then fixed his steely gaze on his wife and told her to mind her own business. Given the abundant and growing evidence, Carole was unable to deny her unsettling feelings; she divorced Gacy in March of 1976. "If there were murders [committed at their residence], some must have taken place when I was in that house," Carole later confided to a reporter.

Once on his own, bachelor Gacy pursued his dark, frenzied passions without interruption. He no longer had to answer to anyone about his late-night adventures. During 1976 and 1977, Gacy killed at least twenty boys and young men, his most prolific run.

Oddly, he also turned his attention to the high-profile political arena, to feed his growing need for attention and recognition. He frequented the Good Luck Lounge on Chicago's northwest side where patrons found him friendly but overly boastful. Gacy befriended a Democratic township committeeman who was impressed with his community service portraying *Pogo the Clown*, entertaining children at local hospitals and birthday parties. Dressed in colorful greasepaint and professional clown garb, Pogo was adored by the children who attended the parties and community gatherings. Gacy won over local leaders, and his political desires became real in 1975. He was named secretary-treasurer for the street lighting commission and served as a precinct captain. Later, Gacy was named director of the annual Polish Constitution Day Parade, and while serving in this role posed for a photograph with First Lady Rosalynn Carter, a photo she surely wishes would vanish.

But Gacy's political career would not last. Rumors about his homosexual interests began to spread after an incident at the Democratic Party headquarters. Gacy, who had volunteered to help clean the offices, was accused of making sexual advances against a sixteen-year-old boy who alleged he had to fight off Gacy's advances with a chair. Gacy apologized and promised not to bother the boy again.

A month later, Gacy again made his move when the boy visited the Gacy home. Gacy convinced the naïve boy to put on handcuffs to learn how to escape from the restraint device. Once Gacy believed the boy was fully cuffed, he began to unbutton his shirt, but the boy was able to slip one hand out of the cuffs and wrestle Gacy to the ground, turning the tables and handcuffing his assailant. Gacy quickly apologized for his crass behavior and promised not to touch the boy again if he would unlock the cuffs. For reasons unknown, the boy unlocked the cuffs and continued to work for Gacy.

For a while, another Gacy employee named David rented a room in the madman's home. David saw a new side of the killer one evening when he came home to find Gacy drunk and outfitted in his colorful Pogo the Clown costume. According to David, Gacy was giggling like a child, and suddenly he stopped. It was dead quiet. Gacy's eyes darkened, and the mood had changed as if a light switch had been flipped. Gacy looked at his employee and growled like an animal, lunging at him yelling, "I'm going to rape you!" David raced out of the house and wisely ended his rental arrangement, remaining one of the few young men to have escaped Gacy's deadly rage.

Gacy's last murder victim was his undoing. In the fall of 1978, he visited suburban Nisson Pharmacy one evening to take measurements for the upcoming installation of several shelving units. While there, he eyed a young employee Robert Piest, fifteen, as the boy busily stocked shelves in the same aisle where Gacy was working. The two spoke briefly, and that appeared to be the end of the encounter until Piest vanished after he punched out at nine o'clock.

Once off duty, the boy told his mother, who was waiting in the pharmacy to give him a ride home, that he had to talk to a man about a job and would return momentarily. Soon, a half hour had passed, and his mother grew more worried with each passing minute. *What could be keeping that boy?* she wondered. It was her birthday, and the family would celebrate as soon as she and Robert returned home. The mother alerted the pharmacy manager who quickly helped her search the store and surrounding area, but they found no sign of the teen.

Mrs. Piest reluctantly returned home thinking her son had gone out with a friend, but it was so unlike him to not tell his parents where he was going. Robert was an honor student and school athlete from a well-regarded family. He always kept his folks informed of his whereabouts. A few hours later, after Robert failed to return home, his mother notified the Des Plaines Police Department, and Lieutenant Joseph Kozenczak was assigned the case. When Kozenczak discovered Gacy was one of the last people to see the Piest boy, he called the killer's home. Gacy gave an excuse why he could not visit that evening, citing a death in the family, but promised to come to the station the next morning to give a statement.

When he finally spoke with police, Gacy denied knowing anything about the missing Piest boy. The seasoned Kozenczak was suspecting the worst when a police background check confirmed his suspicions. Once he discovered Gacy had served prison time for sodomy in Iowa, he obtained a search warrant for Gacy's home. Inside, police found the wallets and driver's licenses of missing boys, class rings, child porn literature, a pair of handcuffs, police badges, an eighteen-inch rubber sex toy and a receipt for a roll of film left for processing at Nisson Pharmacy, Piest's employer. A co-worker had seen Piest place the film receipt in his pocket the night he disappeared.

Inside the trunk of Gacy's car police found pieces of hair later identified by forensic specialists as Piest's. (Later, police would learn the boy had been murdered within hours of leaving work. And the following morning Gacy lay in bed making business calls as Piest's corpse lay stuffed between the bed and a wall.)

Police began to apply psychological pressure, following and observing Gacy nonstop for more than a week, nearly driving the exhausted killer to suicide. Gacy was finally arrested at a gas station for illegal possession of marijuana and taken into custody. Police had finally contained him. Sensing the ever-tightening police noose, Gacy confessed and gave police a detailed hand-drawn map of the crawl space showing the locations of the many bodies buried beneath his house. It appeared the killer was highly organized in all things dark and devious, but the long killing spree was finally over. On December 21, 1978, Gacy was formally charged with the murders.

The body of Robert Piest, his last victim, wasn't found until the following April in the Illinois River southwest of Joliet. According to autopsy reports, the boy had suffocated after Gacy stuffed a large wad of paper towels deep into the honor student's throat.

Gacy's murder trial began on February 6, 1980 and ran for five weeks. More than one hundred witnesses were called to the bench offering a diverse number of assessments of this depraved killer. One witness found him charming and generous. Another witness described the abuse Gacy suffered at the hands of his father for so many years, as he was continually called "dumb and stupid." A Gacy neighbor testified how friendly Gacy had been, calling him a "very brilliant man." Gacy seemed to be a human mirror of what others wanted to see. But the truth was chilling.

"People to Him Are Inanimate Objects."

Dr. Helen Morrison, a psychiatrist for the defense, would eventually spend fourteen years interviewing and studying the madman. She recalled one of her first contacts with the killer. Just before Christmas, Morrison and her husband, newly married, were settling into their new apartment. She was at the kitchen table one evening going through the mail, an assortment of Christmas cards, medical journals and advertisements. One envelope bore handwriting she didn't recognize. Inside, she found a crude handmade card with artwork drawn in pen and crayon. The inscription read, "Peace on earth. Goodwill to men... and boys." It was signed John Wayne Gacy. He had found Morrison's unlisted address and mailed the card from jail. It was a chilling moment; the card a bold, boastful and arrogant statement—just like John Wayne Gacy.

Among the most unsettling and revealing testimonies at the trial came from Dr. Morrison, a forensic psychiatrist who specialized in serial killers. Having spoken with scores of serial killers, Morrison found traits common to all of them. "They can't relate to people but can play roles beautifully, creating complex, earnest performances worthy of a Hollywood

Oscar. They can mimic anything," she explained. "They can appear to be complete and whole human beings, even pillars of society, but they're lacking a very essential core of human relatedness. For them, killing is nothing. They have no emotional connection to their victims. That's probably the most chilling part of it. Not only do they not care, but they also have no ability to care."

When Morrison began her conversations with serial killers, she typically found them friendly, kind and solicitous, causing her to often question whether they were consumed by disorder. "They're charming, almost unbelievably so, charismatic like a Cary Grant or George Clooney," she wrote in her book, *My Life Among the Serial Killers*.

However, Morrison found that in time these broken and demented human beings begin to psychologically break down as the layer of friendliness and affability gives way to a dark and barren core, devoid of empathy. "When I sit with them for four to six hours at a time, without interruption, everything changes. They cannot maintain their friendly role for more than two or three hours," Morrison explained. At this point, she said, the killer begins to fidget and squirm, and beads of sweat are evident on the forehead as he grows annoyed by the persistent inquiry. In time, she can get a killer to reveal more than he wants to share, but this tedious work takes many conversations over several months.

In court, the seasoned psychiatrist shed considerable light on Gacy's twisted nature and testified she had learned more about Jack, the name Gacy had given his dark side; it was Bad Jack who had done all the killing, Gacy maintained. Jack Hanley was the full name of this alternate persona who lived only in Gacy's mind with John as his willing muse.

Morrison told the courtroom jury a police officer named James Hanley dined at the restaurant where Gacy was employed as a cook in 1971 after he arrived in Chicago. Hanley didn't know Gacy well, but Gacy had studied the lawman from afar and fantasized about him. Gacy considered him to be among the most important people he had ever met. Gacy incorporated Hanley's strong demeanor into his own personality, providing a name for the dark power in his being—Jack Hanley. He liked the sound of it—Jack, a strong name.

In court, investigators testified that Gacy had revealed, "There are four Johns." There was John the contractor, the affable small businessman; John the colorful clown, so popular with the kids; John the glad-handing politician; and Jack Hanley, the deadly maestro of all things evil.

Dr. Morrison found that when Gacy's feelings overwhelmed him the killer's psychological state became very unstable. She painted a portrait of a personality with such minimal controls it was easy for violent behavior to come to the forefront, sometimes very quickly.

"Emotions and feelings changed rapidly for Gacy, and he didn't have enough internal structure to keep track of what was happening, let alone prevent it," Morrison said. "He became disorganized, unable to perceive what transpired in even the most familiar of environments. His perception of others became grossly inconsistent and extremely variable. When I examined Gacy, he was often unaware that he contradicted himself from one sentence to the next," the acclaimed psychiatrist revealed. Gacy had told Morrison that authorities had only found a third of his victims. It was difficult to know whether it was just more brash Gacy hyperbole or the truth.

Most chilling, she gave the jury a glimpse of the world through the mind of John Wayne Gacy, a psychopath with an "incapacity to really relate to other people," despite his ability to somehow persuade others and fit in well in social and work environments.

"[For Gacy] there is no way of viewing another person in their complexity. He did not see people with any sense of reality. They were not well-rounded or complex, and they had no variety of traits and qualities. To Gacy, all people were dumb and stupid. People to him are inanimate objects. They have no life to them," Morrison chillingly concluded.

In terms of his sexuality, Gacy apparently made no distinction between men and women. They were both mere props for his twisted games.

As a witness for the defense, Morrison believed Gacy was legally insane, unable to separate from his mother psychologically and develop his own identity. She said he had frequently projected his internal anger and rage, the product of years of his own abuse, onto his victims, considering them unworthy of life. At that point, Jack would take over.

When all the evidence had been heard, the jury took only two hours to reject the insanity defense and render a verdict of guilty in the deaths of thirty-three young men and boys. Gacy's mother and sisters were stunned. His younger sister told the *New York Times*, "He was a normal person like everyone else," she said. "My mother just can't believe it. All she does is cry. I hope people know we're being torn apart by this. We just can't accept it yet."

Gacy was sentenced to death and sent to Menard Correctional Center in southern Illinois where he was confined for nearly fifteen years during repeated, but failed, appeals of his convictions. His neighbors back in the old Chicago neighborhood found it difficult to accept the reality that stood in stark conflict with their experiences with Gacy. "I still can't believe how John could have done that," a neighbor said.

Gacy's suburban Chicago home was razed in the spring of 1979. The vacant lot quickly became a morbid gathering place for rowdy neighborhood kids and ghost hunters. A new home was later built on the lot and remains a must-see attraction for the occasional news crew or tourist.

On May 10, 1994, Gacy was at Stateville Correctional Center in suburban Chicago for the execution. His final meal was fried chicken, french fries, a Coke and strawberry shortcake. During the meal, prison officials reported Gacy was chatty and "talking up a storm." But the mood darkened once Gacy was strapped to a hospital gurney. Two needles were placed in his arm, and a slow saline drip oozed into his bloodstream. When the convicted killer was asked if he had anything to say, Gacy snarled only three words—"Kiss my ass." Defiant, crude and arrogant to the end. There was no affable and friendly John Gacy evident in this final moment. The mask was off. Bad Jack had stepped forward to have the final word.

In his right arm, a double dose of sodium pentothal quickly put Gacy to sleep. Then, the lethal euthanizing agents—pancuronium bromide and potassium chloride—were administered intravenously. As the liquid death dripped slowly into his vein, Gacy strained, gasped and moaned. His pudgy hands and muscles, complicit in so much death, stiffened then relaxed as his dark, evil heart thankfully gave a final beat and fell silent. The depraved serial killer was finally dead, but Jack the demon who had earlier possessed the killer had departed and moved on in his eternal quest to sow despair, destruction and death.

At three in the morning, just two hours after Gacy had been declared dead, Dr. Helen Morrison, the skilled psychiatrist, received a telephone call in her hotel room. It was time. She was driven to Silver Cross Hospital and was soon standing in the autopsy suite. She watched silently as Gacy's bluish body was removed from a van and placed on an aluminum table, specially outfitted for autopsies. The faucets, spigots and drains built into the high-edged table did their work as the autopsy began. Gacy's trunk was opened with a bold pull of the scalpel, and the internal organs were removed and labeled. It was silent in the autopsy suite as Morrison watched the pathologist conduct his macabre, clinical intrusions into the limp flesh of the madman.

Next, the pathologist activated the electric Stryker saw and cut into Gacy's cranium, removing the top of the skull. Then, the organic mother lode was before them—Gacy's brain. The 1,300 grams of folded grey matter lay there, now inert in death, after having been the source of misery, torment and grief for so long. Dr. Morrison was hoping a visual observation of the brain would help identify some structural anomaly that might explain the killer's behaviors. But Gacy's brain looked like any other.

The pathologist severed connections to the spinal cord and removed the brain, which made a "swooshing" sound as it was removed from the cranium, according to Dr. Morrison. The brain was placed in formalin, which served two purposes; it prevented decomposition of the tissue and firmed up the brain for easier handling. The brain was dissected, and carefully prepared slides were sent to an anonymous pathologist for additional study. Weeks later, his reply came back. In part, it stated little could be learned from a brain independent of the living being. "There's no replacement for the study of a person, one who is alive, in different situations with different stimuli."

Dr. Morrison certainly agreed, acknowledging that "A dead organ is almost like a piece of steak that was once a cow... it doesn't allow you to penetrate the living functions of the organism." Alas, the medical specialists had hit a dead end. John Wayne Gacy's brain wasn't giving up any more information.

At the time of Gacy's execution, he was the worst serial killer in modern American history. George Ridgway, also known as the Green River Killer, overtook Gacy in November 2003 when he admitted to murdering forty-eight women in the Pacific Northwest.

Gacy's legacy includes more than forty books about his dark and evil odyssey, two screenplays, a movie, an off-Broadway play, five songs, thousands of news articles and many documentaries. But even in death, Gacy would continue to make news.

* * *

If our psychic sleuths are correct about the Hannibal incident, it means John Wayne Gacy was killing five years before his murderous Chicago killings began. I can tell you this theory is plausible, as our investigation found that Gacy's darkness was revealing itself when he was only fifteen. Gacy had once told his psychiatrist, Dr. Morrison, that he had first killed at that age. Gacy volunteered no more information, and he was never charged. This shocking admission provides important context, however, for another incident involving a fourth-grade boy who lived in the northwest Chicago suburbs.

A decade before the lost boys went missing in Hannibal, the summer of 1957 was unfolding full of promise and fun. The school year had ended for nine-year-old David Bolton who was happily going on vacation with his mother, stepfather and four sisters. As an active boy interested in sports and girls, he looked forward to a summer getaway at a small mom-and-pop resort on Lake Wandawega, just across the Illinois-Wisconsin border. It was a bargain; cabin rentals were three dollars a night.

"I was as happy as can be. There was a big lake where we could swim, canoe and fish. I took my ball glove along figuring I might play some baseball," David explained.

The 120-acre Lake Wandawega, in Walworth County, was crystal clear and eight feet deep. David could see fish swimming near the bottom; the largemouth bass, Northern pike and various panfish almost begged for a baited hook.

The resort had been developed in the 1920s as people enjoyed more leisure time and greater mobility due to the increase in automobile ownership. People found it easy to leave the cities to enjoy nature. David noticed the camp was surrounded by dense forest and low vegetation. It looked like a great place for many grand adventures to unfold during their weeklong stay, or so he thought.

David made his first friend at the camp as he was walking past the end unit of the wing of six attached cabins, situated all in a row. "Hey kid, how's it going?" came a disembodied voice through the window screen. David struggled to see who it was in the bright sunlight but could only make out a dark figure inside. He would soon learn about the true darkness lurking in this seemingly idyllic place.

The boy came outside and introduced himself as John. He was fifteen, a seasonal worker serving as a busboy, dishwasher and general helper. Like David, he was from the Chicago area. "John noticed my ball glove, so we talked baseball, and then he offered to take me in the rowboat. It was my first time, so I was pretty excited," David remembered.

John rowed the boat through the smooth, clear water, maneuvering away from the cabin area and toward a large tree branch that arched over the lake. "He let me row a bit and offered to show me how to catch frogs. John said, 'If you move slowly and remain quiet you can sneak up on them. You'll see.'"

David always enjoyed exploring pond life back home and catching the warty, greenish brown frogs with their bulbous eyes. He liked how they peered across the water's surface, snatching a mosquito or fly with their long, sticky tongues.

John took the oars again and maneuvered the boat near a fallen branch where several frogs were sitting in the dappled sunlight filtering down through the leaves. On the surface of the water, a milky-gray cloud of frog eggs and tiny tadpoles was evidence of a healthy habitat for generations of the harmless, amphibious lake dwellers.

John moved slowly, withdrawing his pocket knife, and with a preternatural swiftness, plunged the blade into the mottled back of one of the helpless creatures. Then another, and another, and another, as his arm arched swiftly and precisely in what was clearly a practiced stabbing gesture. His eyes were wide, tongue hanging out amphibian-like, growing more excited with each lethal swipe of the knife.

David was shocked by the senseless display of brutality on this quiet and beautiful summer morning. "He killed several frogs then handed the knife to me. I told him I didn't want to do that, but he looked me in the eyes and ominously said 'If you don't, I'll drown you in the lake.'"

Reluctantly, feeling powerless to refuse the older boy's order, David killed a frog, as his young soul quietly grieved for the innocent creatures. John happily draped the half dozen frog carcasses across an overhanging limb, displaying their morning kills.

David was now deeply wary of his new friend.

The next day, when John invited David to go on a hike around the lake, the boy was uncomfortable. But, after surveying the area, David noticed the shore was mostly open and visible from the cabin area, so he consented. *What could go wrong*, he thought, trying to reassure himself.

The boys had trekked only about thirty feet, detouring around a dense thicket, when John swiftly turned, forcefully put his hands upon David's shoulders and pushed the boy to his knees. The suddenness of the moves and the change in John's demeanor, so abrupt and unexpected, surprised David who knelt there stunned, his mind focused on the wetness of the morning dew seeping through the knees of his denim jeans.

Then, the quick ripping sound of a zipper coming down, and David's mind began to spin as something firm and fleshy was forced into his mouth. "Do it, or I'll throw you in the lake and drown you. People drown all the time, they'll think it's an accident," John threatened. The sexual assault was over in fifteen seconds, and young, innocent David struggled to understand the calamitous, psychological trauma that had just taken root deep in his psyche.

Life had suddenly taken a dark detour. The memories of this idyllic summer getaway had been replaced by a sexual trauma that would haunt David for decades. "I didn't tell a soul," David sadly explained. "John seemed so friendly and jolly at first, but he was a master manipulator. He knew I'd stay quiet about what happened."

David was happy to see the family's day of departure arrive. On the drive back to Chicago, David's mother turned to the backseat smiling and told him, "That John is a nice young man. I gave him our address so he could visit." Time suddenly stopped, as David froze in a panic. His heart raced as he processed his mother's words, imagining a life where he could be again preyed upon by that demon. "Thankfully, I never saw him again," David said relieved.

In the years immediately following David's childhood attack, he struggled to pay attention in school. He dropped out of high school at seventeen and joined the navy, serving two tours in Vietnam. "My personal outlook on life was pretty bleak. I never had much confidence in myself," David admitted. "But in the service, I was surprised to discover I had the highest IQ in my unit."

While overseas, he received only one letter from his emotionally-detached mother. "I wasn't terribly surprised. She never once told me that she loved me," David sadly shared. "My stepfather didn't like me. Thankfully, my sisters wrote warm and supportive letters to me."

When David came home, he married a young woman he'd met before shipping out to Vietnam, but the relationship soon failed. David was still struggling with post-traumatic stress, only made worse now by his war experiences. "We were arguing all the time. Finally, I told her I can't take this, so we divorced."

The following years were rough as David began to drink heavily to cope, but he finally recognized self-medication with alcohol was no solution.

Breakthrough

Years later, on the day John Wayne Gacy was executed, May 10, 1994, the traumatic childhood memory suddenly and unexpectedly clarified into a crystalline truth for David. As he looked at the face on the television screen, he realized the John at Lake Wandawega summer camp, his sexual attacker, was John Wayne Gacy. He knew in his gut. It all made sense. John was stocky with a round face, just like the adult Gacy. The killer was born in 1942 so he would have been fifteen when David visited the camp in 1957.

David grew bolder, desperate to know more. He pulled out the thick Chicago phone directory and called one of the Gacy prosecutors, attorney William Kunkle, who took the call and shared an interesting bit of news with David. As a teen, Kunkle explained, Gacy had worked at various Wisconsin resorts in the Lake Wandawega area as a busboy, dishwasher and general "gopher." David finally knew the identity of his attacker; after all these years he had a name for the face that had haunted him for nearly four decades. But he continued to bury the memory.

Finally, he connected with a skilled psychologist at the Hines Veterans Administration Hospital in suburban Chicago. "She was persistent in digging down into my past to discover the root cause of my issues." In 2012, she succeeded in bringing the child molestation incident out from a place deep in David's mind. David had never revealed the trauma to anyone. Now, he could finally talk about the assault.

David began to slowly heal. He was sixty-five, a long way from his loss of innocence at age nine.

Now seventy-one, David lives a quiet life in suburban Chicago. "I finally have relief thanks to the medications I must take," he said. "When I left Vietnam, I was so jittery. I couldn't be touched. If someone touched me on the shoulder, I'd jump out of my skin. It's taken many years to get over it."

After enduring a lifetime of traumatic memories about his attacker's *evil* touch, David now understands the *healing* power of human touch, a sign of others' compassion, care and concern. "I still think of it every day of my life. I just wish I could erase it. I'm glad he's dead," Bolton acknowledged.

David Bolton was one of the early surviving victims of John Wayne Gacy. Other men have come forward over the years telling similar stories. All of them were likely victims of this serial-killer-in-development, whose dark nature was already preying upon young boys, a full decade before the three Hannibal boys went missing.

It's difficult to understand the mind of a psychopathic killer. That kind of behavior is far from the reality most of us enjoy daily. Gacy's trouble seemed to begin at the same age David Bolton had been when he was assaulted at Lake Wandawega.

As we know, John Wayne Gacy had a stern, dysfunctional father—John Stanley Gacy—who was a strict disciplinarian, believing that by sparing the rod you spoil the child. After work at night, John Stanley would retreat to the basement and drink heavily, emerging hours later full of anger and making John Wayne his whipping boy.

When young John was in fourth grade, he was overweight and non-athletic. He was bullied by the stronger boys at school where his academic performance soon fell into decline. And his emotional pain only worsened. During his elementary school years, his father's contractor friend would take John for rides in a pickup truck to various construction sites in the area. While away on these drives, the man would sexually molest young John.

Life grew more complicated for the boy. At age eleven Gacy was struck in the head by a swing on the playground. Soon, he was suffering seizures and blackouts which landed him in and out of the hospital several times. The blood clot wasn't discovered until Gacy was sixteen, and once it was dissolved the blackouts ended. A year later, Gacy complained of chest pain and was diagnosed with a heart ailment, but doctors were unable to identify a cause, and Gacy never suffered any heart attack or other complications. Deeply troubled, Gacy finally dropped out of high school.

Feeling the need to get away, Gacy moved to Las Vegas where he worked as an attendant at the Palm Mortuary. In this role, Gacy frequently observed the morticians embalming bodies. Gacy slept on a cot in the embalming room, and one evening he climbed into a casket containing the body of a teenage boy. Gacy held the corpse in a close embrace, caressing the body. Then, apparently unnerved by his own aberrant behavior, Gacy suddenly quit his job and returned to Chicago where he enrolled in a local business school. After graduating in 1963, he took a position with the Nunn-Bush Shoe Company, which would soon lead to the Springfield chapter of his career and later Waterloo.

Demons May Enter Through Shock or Illness

After all of the childhood trauma he had sustained, one has to wonder if the teen years was the period when young Gacy suffered a split of his psyche enabling another personality, Jack, to emerge. Christian experts in demonic possession say demon spirits can take advantage of a weakened area of the mind and personality. Traumatic experiences, they say, may fracture the natural defenses allowing a demon spirit to enter the person.

It was at the age of sixteen, in 1958, that John began to show signs of mental illness, according to Dr. Morrison.

Years later, once Gacy had begun his murderous rampage in the Chicago area, he would drive around and offer rides to young men and boys, take them to his basement or garage, and ply them with alcohol and marijuana before sodomizing and strangling them. And while in Chicago, he operated a small construction company, just as his father's abusive friend had done.

Gacy appeared to be modeling the behavior he had witnessed as a boy from both his alcoholic father and his sexually abusive friend. The killer's psychopathic behavior had become a dark echo of his own childhood, only he went one step further adding the fatal finale. Fueled by drugs and an odd sexual rage, and utterly devoid of any human empathy, he snuffed out the lives of at least thirty-three young men and boys as their lives were just beginning. And he did it as mindlessly as swatting a mosquito.

Now, three psychics are about to begin a northeast Missouri search for a grave, as Gacy's victim count, they claim, grows by three.

Chapter 8
Astonishing Revelations

In mid-August, my brother Brad and I left Minneapolis and drove to Hannibal to begin an extraordinary experiment with the three psychics, Cat Hunt from southern Missouri, Britney Buckwalter from Hannibal and Mary Riley from rural Wyoming.

After spending much of my childhood in Hannibal and having driven northeast Missouri many times during my life, I know the area well. My plan was to take each psychic on independent driving tours of the area to see what they might sense. The goal was an ambitious one—to identify where Gacy took the boys after their abduction, to torture and kill them, then dispose of their bodies. It was a bold, needle-in-the-haystack approach, but we had to know more.

At times it was hard to believe that we were pursuing such an astonishing story. It seemed so unreal, so surreal. But the growing body of convincing evidence was impossible to ignore, no matter how shocking the information. We finally had a chance to find the boys and close the book on this terrible and mysterious chapter in Missouri history.

What would the psychics reveal as we traveled the Hannibal area during the three separate trips? Would the information be conflicting, which I must admit was my expectation, or align in such a way that it would be impossible to dismiss as mere coincidence? Never one to give much thought to paranormal matters in the past, I was slowly becoming a wary and cautious believer in the remarkable ability by a few to look beyond the veil and see amazing things unseen by most other people. I admit I don't fully understand the phenomenon, but I believe these mediums are highly credible. I have confidence they accurately revealed information from the unknown realm, but I cannot be 100 percent certain of its source, which I'll explain in a later chapter.

These women are sincere, humble and faithful. None of them seek attention for what they do to help others. Having heard the incredible information they channeled from beyond, it was time these psychic sleuths were tasked with the big challenge—to prove themselves.

On August 15, Brad and I met Britney at the Mark Twain Dinette, located at the north end of downtown, just below the famous Cardiff Hill, capped by its historic lighthouse overlooking the half-mile-wide Mississippi. Cardiff Hill was named by Mark Twain after a favorite, scenic location he visited in Wales. The dinette is a long-time fixture in Hannibal, famous for its signature loose-ground-beef Maid-Rite sandwich, giant tenderloin on a bun, and ice-cold root beer.

We were seated and perusing the lunch menu when Britney came bustling in a few minutes later smiling broadly. She was wearing a patterned sleeveless dress, sandals, a bracelet on one ankle, a nose ring in her right nostril and a large tattoo covering her left forearm, the handiwork of her husband who is a talented tattoo artist. After our greetings, she got right to the point, again describing what she had channeled during her reading with Denise a few months earlier.

We order lunch and continue discussing the day's plan to drive the area and ascertain what she senses about where the abduction, torture and murders had occurred. Between bites of her BLT, Britney reveals she had seen two numbers during additional channeling sessions—twelve and twenty-one. "Does that mean anything to you?" she asked. I thought for a moment and then realized the possible significance. John Wayne Gacy had been taken into custody by Cook County Sheriff's deputies on December 21, 1978.

After lunch, we pile into my SUV and drive south on Third Street, which soon becomes State Highway 79. Ironically, we drive Britney past the Murphy's Cave hill, but she feels nothing related to the boys at this location. Moments later, the ribbon of highway takes us over the roadbed cave system three blocks south. Again, she feels nothing related to the boys, only the considerable vibrational energy she says is present in all cave systems.

Driving south on State Highway 79, along the western shore of the Mississippi River, we are paralleling the Lincoln Hills, a series of high, picturesque bluffs and hills that stretch from Hannibal southward to Lincoln County north of St. Louis. These hills, with all their scenic splendor, largely escaped the effects of the ancient glaciers that pushed through northeast Missouri half a million years ago, resculpting the landscape.

We will drive nearly fifty miles before this afternoon ends rather dramatically. It's not long before we see results on our driving tour. I turn off Highway 79 onto Fulton Avenue and make a quick right at Bluff Street, which also was called River Road years earlier because the narrow, isolated road parallels the Mississippi. The road is directly below Lover's Leap on the east side of the scenic bluff.

I drive slowly as Britney concentrates; the only sound is the low, soft drone of the air conditioner fan. We travel six-tenths of a mile when Britney suddenly says, "Passed it!" I stop and back up several yards.

Bluff Street/River Road, Gacy's route out of town. Photo by John Wingate.

"We were here," she says, channeling Billy. "I was going to go home." Britney says the conversation in Gacy's car was "...super friendly. The boys trusted him."

Soon, the demeanor changes. "This isn't the way home," Britney says, echoing what she senses from Billy Hoag. "Where are we going?" "We're taking a shortcut," Gacy said according to Britney, now deeply focused with her head tilted downward.

"I feel like this is where the sh*t hit the fan. I feel like this is where the boys were really worried. 'Oh my God! No! You missed our turn!'" Britney says the boys were terrified. "This is where they realized they were in trouble, the place where the boys recognized they had really messed up," she explains. "My heart is racing," she adds, clearly distressed.

A short distance later, Britney sees Gacy pull a white cloth or rag from behind him or from under the seat, not fully understanding its significance at the moment. It soon makes sense.

"If the boys were still alive and remaining in the car, they must have been rendered unconscious. I saw a rag. I saw that several times," she says moving her hand to cover her nose and mouth. Gacy apparently had used a chemical, likely chloroform, to subdue one or more of the boys, just as Mary had sensed on July thirteenth.

She turns her attention to John Gacy. "He is very energetically draining," she laments, adding "He didn't want to keep them long. He was just as scared as the boys were. He's wondering *what am I going to do with these three kids?*" Britney explains that Gacy was nervous, feeling as if he'd taken on too much. "I feel like this night was the first time he killed. I think he had a gun, but I don't think he used it," she reveals.

"I feel like I want to get on Highway 79 and go south," she says anxiously and with urgency. Britney is fully immersed in this supernatural drama as I look back and forth at her and the road, wondering what on earth the next few hours will reveal.

Since Bluff Street is no longer continuous to the Saverton area seven miles away as it once was, we double back around the Lover's Leap bluff and head south on Highway 79, driving right over a portion of the Lost Boys Cave system that made national headlines fifty-one years earlier.

As we're driving, Britney becomes more animated as she focuses on the beyond. "As we're driving south, my heart is starting to race again. We're on the right path. This is where they went!"

Britney falls back into channeling Billy, giving voice to what she's picking up. "We're going to get in trouble! Gonna get in trouble! Turn around, turn around! This isn't right!"

By now, on the evening of May 10, 1967, Britney says the boys knew something dreadful was unfolding, putting them in severe jeopardy. "I'm terrified. I'm starting to sweat, and I'm just overwhelmed," she reveals, glancing at me from the front passenger seat.

The farther south I drive, the more intense Britney's feelings grow. We pass the turnoff to Mark Twain Cave and see the river on our left and high limestone cliffs on the right. The rocky face soon gives way to a wooded area. Suddenly, Britney perks up. "Wait, what's this? I want to go in there," she says pointing to the west. I turn off Highway 79 onto a gravel lane that curves north briefly, then west into a small meadow. Beyond are woods in a valley spanning a hilly area near an electrical powerline corridor.

Suddenly, a large deer steps out of the woods. I point out the doe, and Britney and my brother Brad suddenly see two smaller deer nearby. The three deer stand placidly staring at us. Britney immediately sees significance in the wildlife sighting. "This is definitely a sign, validation that we're on the right track," she says.

I feel a little unnerved as I watch the staring deer, seemingly unconcerned by our presence. This is probably just a coincidence, I tell myself. There are lots of deer in these woods. Still, I can't shake the unsettling feeling that we've arrived at a special place.

We exit the SUV and walk into the meadow. I notice this area is unseen from the highway. "Something happened here. The hair on my arms is standing straight up," Britney says matter-of-factly. "I definitely feel like something went down here, probably a little bit further back into these woods. I'm feeling like this is the spot, although the location of the turnoff from the highway has changed over time. Based on how I feel intuitively and what I'm feeling from Billy, this is definitely where it happened. This is probably where the deaths occurred."

Britney walks farther west toward the woods. "When I first got out of the car, I felt this excitement. Gacy was so excited, so ready," she adds. "I feel like I'm picking up on a mixture of both their energies. Both Gacy and the boys were nervous. When I'm picking up on them all, it gets really hard for me to talk and breathe easily. The weird thing about it is I'm also getting a giddy feeling, which makes my skin crawl. It's like excitement from Gacy. This is it! Let's do this!"

Psychic Britney Buckwalter at the Three Deer Site in Ralls County.
Photo by John Wingate.

Britney looks around, scanning the woods as she gives voice to her feelings and thoughts. "I don't want to be here... my stomach hurts." Britney walks further back into the trees, instantly sensing two of the boys were sexually molested by Gacy. "I'm shaking. My legs are physically shaking. I'm just disgusted. The visions that I'm seeing are not shareable,"

Britney says as she looks around at the trees then back at me, a pained expression on her face.

She tells me that Craig Dowell and Joel Hoag were "treated differently" than Billy. The two older boys were sexually abused, but Billy was spared this particular form of sexual mistreatment. "He couldn't do to Billy what he wanted to do. He wanted the two older ones."

Britney senses from Gacy that he didn't want to keep the boys long. "He's so energetically draining," Britney again complains.

"I know that Billy was hit over and over and over again. Because I'm connecting most with Billy, that would probably be where my headache is coming from. 'He hit me, he hit me!' I want to bend over and grab my stomach because it hurts so bad," she says. "It's so heartbreaking to hear Billy's voice. It just makes my skin crawl to be here. I don't want to be in this place."

Suddenly, Britney directly connects with Gacy. "He says he didn't want to keep them long. I feel like Gacy was on a timeline. He's telling me he stopped, got rid of them, like he was scared to get caught. I'm picking up on the trunk, one boy lying on top of the others. I think they're all in the same place."

Britney again sees the name Jack. "I see it repeatedly," she again reminds me. Gacy, of course, would later acknowledge that he had multiple personalities, and the evil killer inside him was named Jack.

By nightfall, Britney says Gacy had completed his terrible deeds just over two miles from the roadcut area where the boys had last been seen earlier that fateful evening.

"Do you sense where the bodies might be located?" I ask. Britney is not completely sure the boys are buried at what we have dubbed the "Three Deer Site," the location where she says they were tortured and killed. "I think he may have taken them to a different location. He wouldn't have had time to do it here. I feel like he did what he did and got the heck out of here."

We continue driving south to ascertain what else Britney might sense. She keeps seeing the word marble and the letters TT, and we soon understand the significance. Highway 79 goes over Marble Creek, and Route TT is the county road to the small town of Ashburn, population fifty-one. We are now about eighteen miles south and east of the Three Deer location.

After driving through Ashburn, we enter the Ted Shanks Conservation area, a huge wooded area encompassing thousands of acres along the Mississippi River in Pike County. In 1967, prior to development of this state conservation area, the acreage was densely wooded and not as widely available for public access as it is today.

Britney Buckwalter with author in the Ted Shanks Conservation Area.
Photo by Brad Wingate.

We enter the conservation area and turn left onto a white gravel road. Soon the road intersects another gravel road with a posted sign reading "Maintenance Shop—Authorized Personnel Only." We stop and get out of the vehicle and look at the dense woods beyond the road.

"I feel something here. It was dark when Gacy killed and buried them. I feel like I want to bring a shovel and start digging," she says, reacting to the strong energy she's feeling.

I ask whether it would have made more sense to bury the boys where they were murdered in the remote, wooded Three Deer area rather than risk driving them down Highway 79 and through Ashburn to the conservation area. She acknowledges that she could be sensing something else here at the conservation area... perhaps.

Back in June 2003, the body of a thirty-year-old man who had gone missing two months earlier was found in the river beyond the nearby boat access ramp. The man's body was inside his truck in fifteen feet of water. There was evidence of a single gunshot wound, and while authorities suspect it was a suicide, others remain unconvinced to this day. Could Britney be picking up on this death? It's possible, she admitted, adding that the boys could have been buried at the Three Deer Site where she sensed they were tortured and killed.

We had a lot to ponder as we left the conservation area and headed north on Highway 79. Soon we were back in Hannibal, the first phase of our experiment completed. It had been an extraordinary and very revealing afternoon.

As we bid goodbye to Britney, Cat Hunt was already en route to Hannibal from her home in southern Missouri. We would be driving her on a tour of the area early the same evening.

We met Cat at the Mark Twain Dinette about six thirty. At age twenty-seven and sporting a ponytail and glasses, she is ready for the tour, having thought about this unusual story for much of her life.

We drive south on Third Street and cross the viaduct over Bear Creek to Hannibal's southside. We drive past Murphy's Cave, and Cat feels nothing. Our route around Hannibal's southside soon brings us to Bluff Street, the old River Road, the location where Britney sensed the boys had first felt they were in trouble. As we drive, Cat concentrates and keeps her eyes looking ahead, periodically gazing at the trees and brush that's overgrown the shoulders of the old lane. She has no idea we had driven this area earlier with Britney. She and Britney have never met. In fact, they know nothing about each other.

"I see the boys happily running down the side of this road. I feel like they sometimes played in this area," Cat reveals. "Then, there are certain spots along this road, as we drive, that almost make me sick to my stomach. I'm feeling a dread... things are just not good. At first, I felt the boys were happy, but the more we drive, the worse I feel."

"So, the farther south we drive, the worse the feeling gets?" I ask. "Yes," she replies.

I'm shocked at the validation she has just given to Britney's channeling hours earlier. Both women had sensed the same emotional dread at the same location on this isolated stretch of the old River Road.

Cat wants to drive south, so we again take Highway 79, again chasing the scenic hills and woodlands. We pass the turnoff to Mark Twain Cave, and my mind briefly goes back to a childhood memory that has flickered to life.

As a Cub Scout in the summer of 1962, my den-mates and I hiked west of Mark Twain Cave to place birdhouses we had built as a scout project. We parked at the cave and hauled our rough-hewn birdhouses with their postcard-sized, slanted roofs out of the trunk and placed them in our knapsacks. We shouldered our packs and canteens and trudged down a tire-rutted dirt lane that went beyond the cave complex to a large quarry dotted with low scrub. As kids, we joked that this was the road to Mars. It was silly imagining by children with their eyes on adventure as the space program was taking off in the early 1960s.

Walking along in the summer heat, my head was down as I looked for anything of interest. Suddenly my eye caught the edge of something that seemed unnatural in this remote, undeveloped place. I hunched down and plucked a small piece of stone half buried in the dirt. It was an Indian arrowhead that had ended up here by circumstances unknown. Perhaps it had fallen from an Indian's belongings a thousand years ago or slipped from the carcass of a dead deer or rabbit. The point was a modest lithic artifact, perhaps two inches long by half as wide. It had a base that was wide at the bottom but narrowing to two barbed protuberances on each side of the sharpened blade. I beheld it in my hand and called my dad over to have a look. We admired it briefly before I tucked it in my pocket, another addition for the coffee can of fossils, bones, rocks and other earth treasures back in my bedroom.

We trudged onward and found several groves of trees along the periphery of the dusty plain. We each claimed a tree and nailed our birdhouses to the trunks about four feet up. The boys agreed it was good to improve the habitat along one of the nation's busiest bird migration routes, the mighty Mississippi River flowing less than a mile to our east.

We took a break, munched on peanut butter sandwiches and drank from our canteens as we soaked up the quiet. Along the wooded edge of the plain, we gazed out on the dappled area, lovely in its own way, listening to the sounds of the birds and bugs. Then, we gathered our things and headed back. I was soon startled by something at the edge of our dusty path, missed on the approach hike in earlier. Investigating further, I discovered an animal skull with two large eye sockets, most likely a raccoon, and bleached unnaturally white by the harsh sun. I scooped it up, showed the find to the other guys and tucked it into my pack, pleased with the nature find.

The nice memory retreats, giving way to the present, and I think how Joel Hoag would have loved that hike. Although he was not in our scout pack, we regularly explored the hills together. Like me, Joel loved the outdoors and was an enthusiastic amateur naturalist. He would have appreciated the day and my natural history finds.

Now, on this summer evening more than fifty years hence, we are looking for something much more significant—the fate of Joel, Billy and Craig. Cat is deep in an alpha state as her mind remains open to energetic vibrations from the unknown realm. I keep my eyes on the road, hands firmly on the wheel, remaining silent with my thoughts as we drive south.

We've traveled a bit more than two miles when Cat's attention is drawn to a wooded area to the west. "What's this?" she asks as her head snaps to the right. "Let's go here." I brake and turn into the entrance to the Continental Cement Company's property. "I feel drawn to this gravel turnoff. Let's go there," she says, as I make an immediate right turn. We are now on the same gravel lane we had traveled earlier in the day with Britney. We are back at the Three Deer Site. Incredibly, Cat had sensed the precise location Britney had identified.

"I just feel a very strong pull up this gravel road," she explains, as we again drive up into the small meadow surrounded by dense tree and brush cover. "Sometimes you get this incessant need, this pull, to go somewhere and look at something to see what's there," Cat adds.

Clairvoyant Cat Hunt at the Three Deer Site. Photo by John Wingate.

We get out of the SUV and walk into the clearing. Cat surveys the surrounding area and walks tentatively toward the trees to the west. "Something happened here. There's something here," she says looking into the woods. "I haven't talked to Gacy, but his would be a very negative energy and that might explain the nausea I'm feeling here right now," she adds.

This is the extent of what Cat psychically senses here on a humid, summer evening, as fireflies dot the darkening woods with their flashing bioluminescence. Given her limited experience as a medium, she's still learning to interpret the energetic feelings from beyond. But we have seen enough for validation. After driving more than forty miles this evening, Cat has sensed something significant at only two locations. As Britney had done earlier, Cat also identified the route Gacy took out of the town with the boys and the same patch of woods a few miles away where both women assert something terrible happened.

Considering the hundreds of square miles in this portion of northeast Missouri, what are the odds both women would identify the identical locations? I ask Cat if she could be influenced by me, if I was aware of a particular location that might be significant. "No, I can't read minds, and I'm not picking up on energy from the living. What I most definitely feel is energy from the other side. And, it's *very* strong here," she explained.

Chapter 9

Deception from the Unknown Realm?

Let no one be found among you who sacrifices his son or daughter in the fire, practices divination or conjuring, interprets omens, practices sorcery, casts spells, consults a medium or familiar spirit, or inquires of the dead. For whoever does these things is detestable to the Lord.

Deuteronomy 18: 10-11

For our struggle is not against flesh and blood, but against the rulers, against the authorities, against the powers of this dark world and against the spiritual forces of evil in the heavenly realms.

Ephesians 6: 12-13 [NIV]

He who is in you is greater than he who is in the world.

1 John 4:4

The remarkable early findings of the Hannibal investigation left me conflicted. On one hand, I had a deep curiosity to know more about how these three mediums had psychically uncovered the hard-to-believe information. Yet, I didn't want to encourage a potentially dangerous interest among the curious about the unknowable supernatural heavenlies. After praying about this, I felt led and obligated to explore and share the biblical implications of what had transpired to this point.

It is no coincidence such a stunning supernatural drama occurred when it did. There is a growing interest in the supernatural and the New Age movement in our culture today. It is a disturbing trend because more Bible-reading, church-attending Christians are expressing an interest in the unknown realm too. It's as if having seen the light—the Divine truth and saving grace of Jesus Christ, the miraculous healings, the fruits of the Holy Spirit and such—they still want more, so they pursue this curiosity about how the *darker realm* feels and operates. What are its promises they so enthusiastically seek?

A PEW research study conducted in 2018 found that 61 percent of evangelical Christians hold New Age views about topics like divination, astrology and reincarnation. In some churches, leaders are even dabbling with dangerous automatic writing to bring forth revelations from entities who may be masquerading as divine players passing along false words of knowledge or incorrect prophetic insights.

In the consumer marketplace, one can easily find *Angel Cards*, a repurposed version of *Tarot Cards*, and an *Angel Board* that operates like the *Ouija Board*, which theologians warn is a gateway for the occult to gain a foothold in one's life. A *Witch Starter Kit* was briefly marketed but later pulled from store shelves, ironically, after complaints were received from witches.

A sobering headline from the October 2018 *Christian Post* reflects this new trend as interest in astrology and witchcraft become increasingly mainstreamed, even among believers:

Witches Outnumber Presbyterians in the US; Wicca, Paganism Growing 'Astronomically'

Surveys conducted by Trinity College in Connecticut found that Wicca has grown significantly from an estimated 8,000 followers in 1990 to about 340,000 nearly two decades later. Approximately 1.5 million Americans identify as Wicca or pagan, exceeding the number of Presbyterians (1.4 million), and the numbers are growing.

What's going on? Christian leaders believe that interest in the occult is tied to our increasingly post-modern humanist society. "The rejection of Christianity has left a void that people, as inherently spiritual beings, will seek to fill," said Christian author Julie Roys. "Wicca has effectively repackaged witchcraft for millennial consumption. No longer is witchcraft and paganism satanic and demonic," she explained. "It's deceptively described as a pre-Christian tradition that promotes free thought and understanding of earth and nature."

This repackaging is troubling because the information can be accepted as truth by individuals with little or no biblical understanding when it is, in fact, false doctrine. This messy faith construct can result in people becoming more vulnerable and falling further into the trap of deception and sin.

"At a time when the world needs a gospel-preaching church more than ever before, the church is trying to romance the world and become more like the world by teaching these New Age type dogmas," said Thomas Horn, a former Assembly of God pastor who now operates Defender Publishing in the Missouri Ozarks. "It's mind blowing how entrenched in darkness not only the nation is, but how that is seeping into the church body as well."

As rejection of Christian beliefs grows, we see behaviors and ideas once condemned now gaining acceptance. New Agers who practice Wicca and paganism have accepted the lie that they can live without the Lord and still have happiness, peace and eternal salvation. It's a story that goes back thousands of years to that moment in the Garden of Eden when Eve was deceived by the devil to believe life would be better outside of God's will. As people increasingly become narcissistic lovers of self, valuing self-centeredness, material accumulations and the feeding of their pleasures, they fall further away from the real truth—the hope we have rests in God's promises and not in earthly circumstances.

When people become boastful, seeking power for themselves in other things, they are prevented from submitting to Jesus's authority. This kind of arrogance is harmful to relationships and society as it can lead to unforgiving attitudes, abusive behaviors and poor self-control.

The Bible says this life is but a vapor. Eternity is a long time. Decide wisely.

"Do not be carried away by varied and strange teachings..." Hebrews 13:9

A further irony is that while many Christians are turning to the supernatural, many New Agers are turning away from the unknown realms after being saved by Jesus and becoming ambassadors for Christ.

Steven Bancarz, co-author with Josh Peck of *The Second Coming of The New Age*, was one of the leading teachers of the New Age movement. He had the big house and fancy car, paid for with a salary that often exceeded forty thousand dollars a month. But Bancarz experienced a powerful Christian conversion and is now a believer who rejects the supernatural thought he once dutifully taught.

"It reached a point where I had to acknowledge the fruitlessness of this type of spirituality in my life. A lot of New Age teachers I associated with were struggling with drug addiction, sexual perversion or other types of awful brokenness," Bancarz explained. "So, I had to start facing my own sin, and I realized that this spirituality was not producing good fruit in me, and I wasn't fit to be god over my own life anymore. I finally prayed a prayer of salvation with my mother, and that opened the door a crack for Jesus to step into my life."

Days later, on his knees in prayer one morning, Bancarz was suddenly surrounded by a radiant, impossibly bright, pure light. He knew God was present. Bancarz says he was instantly converted and set on his current path as a Christian apologist defending Christianity against ideological attack from New Age sources. It was his Pauline moment, just as Paul experienced when confronted by Jesus in a flash of bright light on the road to Damascus, as related in Acts 9 in the Bible. Like Paul, Bancarz became a modern-day apostle. God truly *can* use all things for His good purposes.

Many individuals in these confusing times are adopting a cafeteria-style spirituality where *they* are the deciders of what is truth while ignoring the real authority of the Creator God of the universe. "The New Age is this umbrella term that covers many topics like witchcraft, paganism, astrology, psychics, astral projection and reincarnation," Bancarz said. "These topics all go into this big spiritual bucket that people can draw from and take parts of different religions to suit themselves and create this idol in their mind of God or grow to believe they are self-actualized as gods themselves."

Essentially, the New Age encompasses everything—except Jesus.

Bancarz found deep deception everywhere. During New Age hypnotherapy sessions to regress a person to explore past lives, he says, demons have full access to your mind and consciousness. "They can drive it, project thoughts into it, give you false memories and insert into your mind thoughts and feelings that seem logical and true to make you think these are your past experiences when they aren't," Bancarz said. "The Bible clearly says in Hebrews 9:27, "It has been appointed for each man to live *once* and then to face the judgment. The question is not are they having these experiences, I believe they are, but what is the standard for interpreting [the truthfulness of] these experiences?"

Bancarz sees witchcraft as especially dangerous, even as so many curious souls find it appealing. Why is this? These dabblers may actually witness something happen in the supernatural, see an effect in nature or in the lives of themselves or others. This can seem very empowering initially. They believe if something happened, they're operating within the truth, but they're not.

In witchcraft, followers appeal to the universe to manipulate beings in the spirit world or energies of nature to cast spells or tell the future. In doing so, they obligate God in a specific way to bow to *their* demands. It's like saying abracadabra and expecting the universe to respond to you. In doing so, they treat God as an impersonal force that can be manipulated. The Bible clearly reveals God as a personal God who knows us by name and who knew us before we were born. He decides in His sovereignty if, when and how he will answer prayers. He is not a genie in a lamp open to human manipulation.

God is the *Creator*; the universe is the *created*—His creation. The Bible indicates Jesus is the only way to God. We humans can do nothing to achieve salvation on our own, nor can we ascend to His level. Only God can save us from sin. Believers who repent and come to Christ are washed clean of their sins and enter heaven spotless.

So, what is the end result when a person follows New Age beliefs to the fullest? Bancarz and his co-author Josh Peck offer a clear explanation in their book *The Second Coming of the New Age*:

> If you are your own god, you are as good as it gets for you. No one can help you spiritually, because no one else is your god; only you are. Your limited experience on Earth is all you have to guide you through the mysteries of the universe, death and beyond. You have to figure out how to provide your own afterlife without even really knowing what happens when you die. Choosing to be your own god means you are worshipping a being who cannot create anything new, cannot save you from death, cannot provide you any answers you don't already know, cannot tell you what will happen for you, cannot provide a divine meaning or plan for your life, and cannot understand anything about reality outside of a human perspective.
>
> You are betting your entire existence on being able to navigate the mysteries of the universe through cognitive limitations, sensory limitations and geographic limitations in time and space. Your three-pound brain is the only real reference point you have.
>
> Does that sound reassuring?

A Demonic Plot

Bancarz believes our culture and the church are in a crisis, as belief in New Age ideas grows more rapidly than belief in Christianity. "Many people have this idea that this is just a fringe topic, but this is what's taking over the church. It's not atheism any more, it's New Age spirituality," he explained, "and it's a demonic plot to keep people away from salvation in Christ."

Let's read that last line again. New Age spirituality is a demonic plot to keep people away from salvation in Christ. Now you better understand why Christianity is under assault in our culture, while other faiths like Buddhism or Hinduism are left alone. Satan knows the truth and understands where he needs to focus his resources. While God is the Creator of all that is good and full of life, Satan is the father of lies, intent on sowing as much confusion, deception and destruction as possible.

The wisdom and correctness of Bancarz's decision to seek Jesus was confirmed when some New Agers, having learned of his Christian conversion, taunted him with cries to kill himself. Should we be surprised? As the Bible teaches, you will know them by their fruits.

For many years, Doreen Virtue was the bestselling New Age author in the world. That is until January of 2017 when she had a "life-changing vision of Jesus that caused me to walk away from the New Age," said the author of *The Joy of Jesus*. Virtue says people must seek God for answers, and not rely on humans indoctrinated in practices that may cause them to abandon the church and become more vulnerable to the influences of demons.

Spiritual Battle

So, at this point in the twenty-first century, the spiritual battle is heating up as more people question biblical truth and move beyond scripture to explore the wider spiritual domains. "We are a spiritually hungry people," said Frederick Thoni, a suburban Minneapolis pastor. "Why do these things fascinate us? Why are we drawn to them? Because we want to pull the curtain back and see into the spiritual realm, which we know so little about."

I encountered Pastor Thoni at a University of Northwestern St. Paul staff picnic on a beautiful summer day in late August of 2018. My wife and Fred's wife are on staff at the university. I quickly discerned that it was no coincidence Lynae and I—among the large crowd in attendance—ended up seated at the same table as Pastor Fred and Kai. Though, he may have regretted asking me about the topic of my next book.

As we enjoyed our burgers and potato salad, I leaned in across the cafeteria table that separated us and brought him into the very small circle of those with knowledge of the extraordinary Hannibal psychic investigation. For the next thirty minutes, I shared what we had learned during this amazing summer of discovery in northeast Missouri. He was astonished by the story, and we quickly arranged a time to meet the following week to further explore its biblical implications.

When I visited Pastor Fred's church, we settled into the comfortable Fireside Room, a perfect place for discussion, quiet reflection and prayer. As I related the story of the three missing Hannibal boys and the massive 1967 cave search, he recognized the impact of these kinds of traumatic events in our lives.

"I understand the draw of this story for you," he said. "I had a classmate drown at a class swimming party in high school. Our families were friends. Our dads were childhood friends. That's been a part of my life ever since. You don't forget those things. They're part of who we are. This past summer, I was talking with the sisters of this boy, and as I talked about being at his graveside, the tears came. It was like no time had passed, and this happened in 1971." Pastor Fred understood the power of these traumatic memories experienced in childhood. Such intrusive memories have a way of remaining prominent in our minds, even with the initial shock and emotion present.

Offering context for our planned discussion, Pastor Fred acknowledged that as a teenager, he had dabbled in New Age topics out of a consuming curiosity about the supernatural. "Before I became committed to Jesus, I was reading everything. I was studying Chinese iChing, I was looking at Tarot cards and Ouija-boards. I was so curious, but when I came into a relationship with Jesus, baptized in the Holy Spirit, I suddenly realized there was a world of difference here. The source is not the same. I burned all the books and tapes that I had accumulated, because I finally recognized that I had lacked discernment about all this before becoming a believer in Jesus."

Pastor Fred Thoni.

Later, as a college student, Thoni discovered the dangers that come with exploring dark supernatural realms. He came face to face with a demon who had taken possession of a young woman with much sin in her life due to poor life choices. The chilling supernatural event happened in Madison, Wisconsin, where Thoni was participating in a summer fellowship group. With the presence of God so intense at these Christian gatherings, demons can get stirred up by the Divine presence, and the people who are possessed become very upset and behave erratically. Thoni and several others counseled this woman who agreed to have them pray for her deliverance from this demonic influence that was making life so miserable.

"There was a group of us praying with her. I was inexperienced but believing in the authority of Christ," Thoni explained. "And this demon would *not* leave this woman. You would see it in the manifestation on the woman's face. Her mouth would close, and the head would maniacally shake No, No, No! The demon adamantly refused to leave her," Thoni said.

At times, Pastor Fred explained, the voice coming out of this woman was not her own voice; it was a deep growling one. "It was a demonic voice, taunting us, mocking us. 'You can't make me leave. You can't make me go! I will not go! I have a right to stay here!'"

As the deliverance team had previously prayed for the Lord to give them authority to deliver this woman, they had the wisdom and the Divine equipping to do battle with this cunning and entrenched demonic spirit.

"As we were praying, we had a moment of inspiration from the Holy Spirit to ask the demon, 'Who is your master?'"

The woman's head shook violently back and forth; the demon simply was not cooperating and would not answer.

"I said, 'We command you in the name of the Lord Jesus Christ, name your master!' And with closed, clenched teeth the growling voice uttered, 'Satan!' And then I said, 'Who defeated Satan? Who died on the cross and whose blood defeated him?

Who is it? I command you to name him!' Again, through gritted teeth, the demon finally relented—'Jesus!' Then, one of the prayer warriors boldly commanded, 'In the name of Jesus, leave now!'"

And with a chilling, otherworldly screech, the demon left the woman.

"Do not offer any part of yourself to sin as an instrument of wickedness, but rather offer yourselves to God… as an instrument of righteousness." Romans 6:13

I sat speechless for a moment, astounded that this bizarre story could grow even stranger. Pastor Fred broke the silence, reminding me of a foundational truth about the demonic realm. "We must always remember the devil is a liar and a deceiver from the beginning, and he will use those demons to distract you, to take you down rabbit trails, anything to divert, confuse or harm you."

Indeed, the devil is real and not a metaphor for temptation, sin and the world's evil. Satan is much more than allegory. Pope Francis has stated that Satan, the grand deceiver and seducer, is a literal supernatural being dedicated to debasing and deceiving human beings. In his apostolic exhortation released in April 2018, the pope wrote, "We should not think of the devil as a myth, a representation, a symbol, a figure of speech or an idea." Satan, he described, is a personal being devoted to assailing us whenever opportunity strikes.

Our conversation turned back to the three Christian mediums who had discovered so much new information about the missing boys, John Wayne Gacy and his torture and murders of Joel, Billy and Craig. Pastor Fred made an important point that lends credibility to the women's psychic sensing about the lost boys.

"All three women seem sincere and very perceptive," he said. "They are," I agreed.

Women, Pastor Fred explained, are generally the more intuitive gender. "That's part of women's intuition. In our culture, women are often able to be more perceptive, more discerning, about these things. Women are generally found in greater numbers in church, in bible studies and prayer meetings. And I think this goes back to the uniqueness of the way God made women."

It's an interesting point. If you look at the Bible, from the very beginning of the New Testament period, there were women who followed Jesus along with the disciples. There were women at the cross when He was being crucified. It was the women who first went to the grave to complete the burial process. Later, Mary Magdalene, whom Jesus had earlier exorcized of seven demons, became a first witness of the resurrection, that powerful historic moment when Jesus was resurrected and became the redeeming Christ for the world's believers for all time.

"Follow the source of the power in this Hannibal situation," Pastor Fred counseled, "and see where these modern-day women believers are plugged in at."

* * *

Let's take a moment to look more closely as the spirit realms. We humans are comprised of body, mind and spirit, living in a reality that is both physical and spiritual. But just because something is spiritual doesn't mean it's necessarily of the Holy Triune God. There are other entities lurking in the unknown realms.

When looking at the energetic domains in God's creation, the Christian tradition describes the soul and spirit as two primary immaterial parts of humanity. Humans *are* a soul, comprised of the will, emotions, thoughts and personality that make us who we are. The word soul can be applied to a person, whether alive on Earth or in the afterlife.

We connect with God with our entire being—mind, body and spirit. The spirit is the immaterial part of us that connects with God who Himself *is* Spirit. (John 4:24).

God creates the body then breathes life into each human being. The Hebrew word *ruach* means both spirit and breath of life. When a soul dies, the spirit or breath leaves them.

There are also non-human etheric beings in heaven and elsewhere in the heavenlies. Angels were Divinely created by God even before he created the physical universe. There are angelic beings and the specialized Guardian Angels. These created beings act as God's agents sent to protect and guide a person, group or country in times of need. As John Calvin penned in his inciteful 1536 magnum opus *Institutes of the Christian Religion*, "The angels are the dispensers and administrators of the Divine beneficence toward us; they regard our safety, undertake our defense, direct our ways, and exercise a constant solicitude that no evil befall us."

These angels are not bound by gravity or other earthly physical laws. They are immortal and invisible but can manifest in the human visual field when necessary. They have far greater power than humans, but they are not omnipotent like God. Angels don't marry or have children. While popular culture often portrays angels as feminine figures, the Bible reveals these beings as strong, masculine figures. Devout Christians who have had angelic experiences describe them as seven or eight feet tall and appearing to weigh up to four hundred pounds. It is widely believed that we each have a Guardian Angel to guide and protect us, to aid our intuition, judgment and decision-making, and then to guide the soul into the afterlife. As angels do not sin, they don't need redemption. Nor are there any promotions; they remain in their angelic roles for eternity, busily doing God's work in the earthly realm.

"Angels are mentioned 108 times in the Old Testament and 165 times in the New Testament," wrote Pastor Dr. David Jeremiah in *Angels, the Host of Heaven*. "I find it odd that celestial beings are mentioned so many times and yet are so poorly understood."

What little we do know includes the other types of angels mentioned in the Bible: the cherubim, seraphim and archangels. The cherubim are the heavenly creatures nearest the throne of God serving as courtiers or personal servants. The seraphim are winged beings above God's throne, praising and worshipping God, as identified by the prophet Isaiah, who was given a vision of heaven. The seven archangels, Michael, Gabriel, Raphael, Uriel, Saraqael, Raguel and Remiel, are above angels in the heavenly hierarchy and serve as messengers, warriors, healers or have ministries of mercy, justice, wisdom and repentance.

In Genesis, we read of the rebellion by Satan (believed to have been an archangel) who sought his own greater authority in God's divine heavenly domain. God cast out Satan and one-third of the angels down into the heavenlies where they continue to exist and cause trouble in our lives on earth.

While scripture does not mention the specific number of created angels, the Book of Revelation provides details of a vision by John the Apostle who saw what he described as "ten thousand times ten thousand angels," which totals one hundred million angels. If more than thirty million are fallen angels, there is plenty of potential trouble possible from these beings who are so devoted to confusion, deception and destruction.

We also read in the Bible about human men who supernaturally sensed visions and voices no one else could sense. The major-prophets Isaiah, Ezekiel, Jeremiah, Daniel and another dozen minor-prophets received supernatural communications from God and helped pen the Bible. These were *Holy* encounters with anointed men who heard from God.

Then, we read of Noah who faithfully followed God's instructions and built an ark to save life on the planet when not a drop of water was falling from the sky. Moses had visions of plagues and the deaths of firstborn sons during a desperate search by demonically-animated leaders who were intent on the destruction of the infant Jesus.

The Bible, however, warns believers (Deuteronomy 18:11) about connecting with *familiar spirits*, non-divine entities that are mysterious in origin and can connect with psychics. There are two schools of thought on these spirits. One theory is that these familiar spirits are the vibrational energies of people who have died but remain disembodied human spirits not yet at rest. These spirits need prayer to commend them into the presence of Jesus in heaven, so they stop their wanderings. Another theory posits these spirits are fallen angels or demons masquerading as the souls of the dead to entice contact with humans across the invisible realm during a channeling session or a seance. These demons dwell in the heavenlies or Tartarus, the invisible realm all around us encompassing the earth, the airy atmosphere and the airless void of space. These fallen angels are confined until the day of judgment but remain free to roam with limitations to do their damage in the lives of earth dwellers. As Revelation 12:12 describes, these spirits know the time is short, so they are "filled with fury."

As angry and vengeful spirits, they strive to enter the high places of our culture and influence people in government, politics, education, media/entertainment, the law, finance and sports. When opportunities arise, they seek to enter human beings and possess them to influence their thoughts, will and behavior. Tartarus is a bizarre and unknowable domain, whisper-close to our three-dimensional world, separated only by a thin veil. That's why theologians counsel us not to try to understand it. God, they say, has told us all we need to know in His Word.

Experienced psychics, including our three mediums on the Hannibal case, believe they are in contact with the souls of the dead or other helpful spirits they believe are angels. They claim the ability to easily discern the different vibrational energies to ascertain whether a particular spirit is good or evil in nature, though many Christian theologians are skeptical humans have such ability.

Clearly, channels appear to exist for communication between the physical and non-physical realms, but there are rules. God's kingdom includes both the visible earthly realm and the invisible spiritual plane, and He rules over both domains. Believers are told in Mark 13:23 to take heed and beware of false christs and false prophets who will rise and show signs and wonders to deceive even the elect (Christian believers).

Believers pray in Jesus's name and faithfully know that God hears our prayers. Many believers receive divine insights, Words of Knowledge and prophetic dreams and visions, even today. As inhabitants of this world, we are blessed with periodic examples of heaven coming to earth, such as miraculous healings. The Lord's Prayer instructs us how to best limit our supernatural focus. The adage "As in Heaven, so on earth" is part of the Lord's Prayer we recite as we seek *God's will* to manifest in our world as it does in heaven.

There are limits to supernatural communication across the realms, and the Bible helps clarify this point. In the book of Luke (16:19-31), Jesus talks of the abyss between heaven and hell, "...between us and you there is a great chasm fixed, so that those who wish to come over from here to you will not be able, and that none may cross over from there to us."

There is an interesting biblical exception about divine communications. In 1 Samuel 28, we read about King Saul, dressed in disguise, asking a medium in the town of En Dor to contact Samuel after he had died. There remains a question whether it was actually Samuel that was contacted, but the Bible implies it was his spirit.

Why do we see this exception? No one in this world is certain, but the medium communication may have been allowed for the purpose of rebuking King Saul for sinful behavior, something that does not happen in contact with familiar spirits. Perhaps God provided a learning moment to show us the difference between those who are really of God and those familiar spirits not divinely appointed.

This passage can be interpreted several ways, according to theologians:

*God, indeed, caused the woman to see the spirit of Samuel.

*Another view is that the woman contacted an evil spirit who imitated and appeared to her as the spirit of Samuel.

*Or, the woman discerned Saul's thoughts and pictured Samuel in her mind. The Bible explains that the woman cried out in surprise when she saw Samuel, perhaps because she wasn't expecting to conjure his spirit.

Whatever the explanation, God enabled her to recognize Saul and warn him of the coming battle with the Philistines that would result in his death.

* * *

Source of Power?

So, given the complexities of the spiritual realms, what is the source of power the three mediums are connecting with? Our three psychic sleuths say they adamantly avoid delving into anything of a dark or satanic nature, confident they can discern such dark vibrational energy. The three Christian women say they merely use the intuitive gifts given them by God, and only after prayerfully seeking God's direction and protection.

But are they connecting with the spirits of the lost boys from heaven and Gacy from hell, other disembodied human spirits not at rest, the Holy Spirit, angels, the protective and helpful guardian angels or something dark and malevolent in Tartarus?

From the beginning of this odyssey, understanding the dangers of this supernatural terrain, I have prayed for God's protection, guidance and discernment. I've not personally engaged in any supernatural channeling or readings. I've merely been an independent observer of these extraordinary happenings. I've witnessed these three women—independently—reveal the same criminal scenario and identify the same locations where they say three boys were abducted, tortured, murdered and buried.

From the earliest moments, I've wondered—if this is all true—whether the whole drama was a Godly fruit. We know that God can use all things for His good. Could His hand be guiding these mediums to finally solve this mystery and bring closure to a half-century of grief and trauma felt by so many individuals? Could He be revealing to us that Gacy's killing started much sooner than historically understood? Or, could all of this be the work of trickster spirits, fallen angels desiring to sow false hope and despair on top of a half-century of sadness and trauma?

I posed the question to Pastor Fred Thoni. "Could this be a God thing?"

"You and these women may very well be called for just such a time as this, to help bring healing and closure. I wouldn't discount that. It could certainly be the Holy Spirit conveying this information," Thoni acknowledged.

"Scripture, in the book of Matthew, tells us to look at the fruit, through the submission to the authority of Jesus Christ. Look at the fruit of these women's lives. When they pray to God, do they really seek to love and honor Christ, or are they just naming him in name?"

I tell Pastor Fred that Mary, Britney and Cat maintain they are faithful Christians who pray to the Lord prior to conducting a reading. All three are sober, mature women who don't seek attention for their supernatural crime-solving work. All three told me they have never encountered anything demonic while doing their work, with the exception of the dark, exhausting energy they felt was John Wayne Gacy. His was a dark energy they clearly felt.

The psychics, I tell him, spoke with conviction when they told me they channeled the energy of the three lost boys from heaven and Gacy from hell, adding they can tell the difference in vibrational energy patterns among spirits and believe this type of communication is possible between our world and the other realms.

Cat saw the boys' energetic spirits manifest at my book signing event, evolving from energetic orbs of light into more etheric human forms. Britney sensed Gacy's darkness but also connected with the three boys who identified Gacy and revealed they were beaten and strangled. She heard what she believed to be Billy Hoag's boyish voice. Mary connected with Gacy, Craig Dowell and Joel Hoag, who showed her the Lover's Leap area and the part of the route they drove the day they vanished. Gacy, with evil pride, had revealed his shameful, torturous deeds in the wooded area south of Hannibal. And during this odyssey, the women had additional supernatural assistance, they say, from other "helpful" intelligent spirits.

"In the case of these three women," Pastor Fred said, "I don't discount what they have said, what they are sensing, what

146

they believe and perceive... I'm not questioning that. They're not sensationalistic people just making up something."

The danger, he pointed out, is that we as mere humans cannot know with *certainty* whom we are communicating with across supernatural realms. Could these women sincerely believe they are connecting with the three boys and Gacy when, in fact, they are channeling something else? Is it impossible for us to truly know with certainty the source of such information?

Given the potential for demonic deception, we must consider the possibility, however remote, that this entire experience could be demonically orchestrated, as Pastor Thoni suspects. The reader can now better understand why the Holy Bible forbids believers from pursuing supernatural New Age practices. It is an unending rabbit hole that can confuse and harm human souls. Still, it's ironic that one reason some people pursue an interest in the New Age and the spirit realm is because the Bible tells us so little about it.

I share the Pastor's additional comments in totality because they are so gripping and relevant to this story:

> **Q:** Can humans, even believers, so easily be fooled into believing something evil is good?
>
> **A:** We know from scripture that sometimes Satan is perceived as an angel of light. He doesn't always come as a red-faced demon with a forked tail, horns and a pitchfork. Sometimes, he manifests as a brilliant, magnificent creature of light.
>
> **Q:** Is it possible the spirits of deceased humans can manifest into our plane of existence to provide information?
>
> **A:** Let's look at Gacy. There is something demonic around the energy of this man, his energy. What

is that? What is it these women are sensing? I believe they're perceiving a tremendous surge of evil coming towards them, against them. Is this a dead man whose spirit is roving around and able to manifest in this way? Or is it something else? Personally, I believe the dead are dead, and that they don't have the ability to roam around as spirits.

Q: So which entities might psychics be connecting with across the unknown realm?

A: From a biblical perspective, there is what scripture identifies as familiar spirits, and these are demonic spirits—demons—that are part of the demonic host under the authority of Satan. They are his minions or emissaries to do evil in this world. I don't believe these women have directly encountered the spirit of this vile, sinful man Gacy. He was executed and died in 1994. But there were demonic spirits around him during his life, very possibly inspiring him, motivating him and manipulating him, even possessing him, to do the horrid things that he did with all those boys and young men.

Q: And these spirits are still around because beyond space/time, 1967 happened only an instant ago, right? To an eternal being, time means nothing.

A: That's right. When Gacy died, these spirits did not die. This is an important point. These malevolent spirits are *still around*. Studies have shown us that where tragic, demonic events have occurred, familiar spirits tend to gather there. It attracts them. It's a place of darkness and evil. So, in the case of Hannibal, it would not surprise me that such a horrendous deed was done to these boys, and it has become a spiritual magnet for demonic forces. And when you bring in individuals who are spiritually sensitive, they begin to immediately sense the presence of some dark force. I don't believe it's Gacy. He's gone and is being dealt with eternally because of his broken, sinful life, but these familiar spirits *are* there, and they *are* familiar. They know every detail of what happened in May of 1967, and they can impersonate individuals who were there at the time. They know all of the details of what happened moment by moment.

Q: This is a chilling scenario to ponder, to know that intelligent evil remains active in a specific area surrounding a specific event.

A: It is my view that these ladies are coming smack dab into an encounter with familiar spirits. And as scripture indicates, there are levels of demonic power, and some of them have more power and authority in the spiritual realm than others, and there may be significant demonic spirits that remain active. They're still involved with all of this.

These words are wise Christian insights from a pastor who understands better than most the dangers and deceptions of the supernatural landscape. His remarks paint an alternative explanation that may be impossible for anyone—even these three experienced and sincere mediums—to fully and correctly discern unless we recognize the authority that is God's Word. Ultimately, this is an issue of Divine authority, because God has given us free will, and a curious nature, yet we just cannot know with certainty the totality of God's creation and how it operates, even the darker realm where the fallen ones lurk. This is, of course, the most frustrating aspect of this story—we are stuck with our own limited human understanding, our fallen nature and individual bias.

"We want answers, but we have to be careful because the devil is a liar," Thoni said. "He's come to rob, steal, kill and destroy. He's out for blood. He doesn't play fair. He will do anything. He will sacrifice anyone, use anyone to manipulate and destroy the testimony of Jesus Christ and the power of Christ in someone's life. He wants to do as much woe as possible."

As discerning Christians, we do not live in fear of Satan. Yet, it is so important that we properly discern the spiritual realm and the spiritual battle, that is as old as humanity, so we are aware of its reality and its subtlety as we proceed through earthly life.

Finally, Pastor Fred and other Christian leaders who are experienced in deliverance tell us that indwelling demonic spirits will take a name, sometimes an everyday name or a spiritual identity. In John Wayne Gacy's case, you'll recall his disclosure to a Chicago detective that his other personality—his demonic nature—took the ordinary name of Jack. It was the name Mary and Britney had sensed repeatedly early in their psychic encounters.

Well, Jack still has something to say.

And the most extraordinary aspect of this story will now be revealed as Wyoming medium Mary Riley takes her turn, traveling eastward from Wyoming for a most astonishing late summer visit to Mark Twain's boyhood hometown.

Chapter 10
Torment in the Woods

Having previously explored Northeast Missouri with two of the psychics as part of this extraordinary investigation, I returned to Hannibal on September 6, 2018 to prepare for the final phase. I would be driving the third medium, Mary Riley from rural Wyoming, around the Hannibal area in our attempt to identify more details about this extraordinary Gacy abduction-murder scenario.

The goal, as challenging as it seemed to me, was to discover if all three women could identify the abduction route and the possible location or locations where the boys' remains might be found. It was a worthy, yet seemingly impossible goal, but with promising results from Cat and Britney, we pressed forward. I still struggled to fully comprehend the strange nature of this unfolding mystery.

As I arrived, the remnants of Tropical Storm Gordon from the Gulf of Mexico had moved north and was pelting much of eastern Missouri with a steady rainfall that would last for twenty-four hours. By Saturday morning, September 8, 2018, the worst of the rain had passed to the east, but heavy overcast remained, and the high humidity hung low like smoke over the forested hills of northeast Missouri.

Mary and Tanner Riley had arrived late the previous night but were ready to go when I met them at the Becky Thatcher Café for an early breakfast. Mary, blonde and blue-eyed, a dance instructor back home, slid into the booth followed by Tanner, tall and laid back, an easy-going rancher who also operates a big excavator shovel at a Wyoming coal mining operation.

"We're finally here," Mary says, excitedly glancing out the window at nearby Cardiff Hill with its historic lighthouse. "It's kind of overwhelming, but there is a peace I'm feeling. It's finally happening, and my energy is really calm," she adds.

"What kind of preparation do you make before a day like we have ahead of us?" I ask.

"Nothing is really set in stone. I usually like some calm music and quiet to start the day, so nothing interrupts my energy," she explains.

While we peruse the menu, I share that Craig Dowell's mother, Helen, was waitressing at the Becky Thatcher Café in May 1967 when the boys went missing. The café has since been remodeled with bright lighting, comfortable booths and plenty of chrome to give the place a 1950s feel, complete with a large Elvis poster hanging on the wall, an incongruent counterpoint to the Mark Twain tourist venues evident around town.

We order and savor our coffee as we get to know each other and discuss plans for the day. Noting that the Hannibal area, and Missouri overall, has many caves, I wonder aloud if that poses a challenge. "Caves hold a lot of energy that I can feel. I was once in a house that sits over a cave, and the energy was very strong. But the caves shouldn't be any distraction today. People and spirits feel different to me," she explains.

I ask her about the intuitive gift she has carried her whole life, a question she hears frequently. "Well, we can't read minds. We're not God," she says with a smile. "I'm a medium, between two worlds, a messenger using the gifts that God gave me."

It's a lot to absorb, she admits, for people firmly rooted in the busy three-dimensional world of everyday earthly life. "Many people have trouble wrapping their minds around something greater than this world."

Indeed. As a Christian, I keep my eye on heaven, but now we found ourselves in the heavenly suburbs with this story, and the rules are very strange and seemingly unfathomable.

We finish our breakfasts and head to the car. As we drive, Mary continues tutoring me on how she believes this medium communication functions across the heavens. As she speaks, I realize that we humans certainly appear to be in a bizarre fellowship with spirits in the realms beyond, if only we could all sense the totality of Creation. These spirits are as much a part of reality as our defined material world. Those with special gifts are able to communicate with the spirit world, she says, but the conditions of life beyond are modified from those we experience here. Communication is different, done through energetic, vibrational feelings and messages projected as thoughts, images, sounds or smells.

What must this be like, I ponder, only to later stumble upon an apt analogy. Take a moment and recall the sound of a deceased loved one's voice. Or, think back to a treasured childhood vacation or other fun memory. You see it in your mind, right? Can you recall any sounds? These examples come somewhat close to giving you an idea what it's like to sense the other side, I'm told.

And this realm may not be far away; perhaps only a curtain, the thickness of atoms of a differing vibrational frequency, separates us from the supernatural. It's always there until that time we seamlessly cross over at death for eternity or initiate communication with the aid of a medium like Mary, Britney or Cat.

Eternity it seems does not start at death; we have been in eternity for our entire lives, this continuum of earthly life to death to eternal life into which we are born. The Bible speaks of us as merely a vapor. Indeed, life on Earth, for those blessed with the gift of many decades, is but a nanosecond compared to the eternity of life beyond.

During her preternatural experiences, Mary has seen angels and guardian angels who specifically protect us and chilling demonic forces like Gacy seeking to destroy us. She has frequent contact with what she calls *intelligent spirits*, the immaterial energetic beings who can respond to questions, provide detailed information and physically move objects in our three-dimensional world. She believes that souls eternally located in heaven are able to energetically connect with our world with the help of attentive mediums. In this place of higher energetic frequency, she says, a whole series of unique dramas can play out.

Sometimes, we can see only one side of these dramas from our limited worldly perspective, as the following example I relate to Mary dramatically illustrates. A family friend, Charles, now retired as a professor of biblical history, once related to me an incident his physician father experienced during his work in northern Minnesota. Doc, now deceased, was a long-time country doctor and a devout Christian. Doc had a patient, Frank, an avowed dyed-in-the-wool atheist who rejected any belief in God. Frank refused to hear any Christian witnessing despite the doctor's best efforts during the span of many years.

One winter when Frank grew gravely ill, Doc tended him and even sat overnight with the patient in his rural Minnesota home. This was in the 1940s when physicians made house calls and did such things.

The winter night was subzero and quiet until about three in the morning when Frank suddenly cried out, "Doc, Doc!" The doctor raced up the stairs and into the bedroom to find the sick man sitting bolt upright in bed, his eyes wide open in terror, as he lamented, "The fire, the flames, it's so hot!"

And once the moment of high drama passed, Frank fell back onto the pillow dead. Doc had seen many miracles in his decades of medical practice, but this supernatural moment was the most soul-chilling ever, as he grieved for Frank's soul.

* * *

After driving to Hannibal's southside, we switch gears to the beckoning subject at hand, our tour. Mary suggests we begin by driving to the former Hoag house. It's a good idea, but as the home was one of several razed in 2006 for construction of the new A. D. Stowell school, we can only visit the general location at Fulton Avenue and Riverside Street. The large, two-story home for the family of thirteen is now just a memory; all that remains on the immediate site is a fire hydrant and a grassy slope leading to the school property.

Mary explains that during her first channeling session in mid-July Joel Hoag had shown her a grocery store that seemed important. At the time, she saw in her mind's eye the letter B followed by four blanks boxes awaiting other letters.

I am stunned by the revelation and quickly understand its significance.

"That's an easy one," I explain, playing a real-life game of Wheel of Fortune. "Burns," I reply. Burns Grocery was a small store located at the same intersection, just catty-corner across the street from the Hoag homestead. The store was operated by the elderly Mr. Burns, whose patience was frequently overwhelmed by the sheer number of youthful, energetic invaders. The store was a popular hangout for neighborhood children who made frequent candy and ice cream purchases.

Although Mr. Burns seemed gruff, he was a grandfatherly figure for the neighborhood kids. When our Cub Scout pack was working on a space program theme for our booth at the annual Scout Jamboree at the Hannibal Armory in the early 1960s, Mr. Burns saved several of his five-gallon ice cream buckets for us to repurpose as space helmets. We cut out an opening for clear plastic face plates and used orange juice cans for the earpieces. Once the whole affair was covered in aluminum foil, we had our convincing head garb for the Jamboree. We all were astronauts, thanks to Mr. Burns.

"Joel is showing me that the store was important. I think they drove by here in Gacy's car." I suggest that, perhaps, this is where the boys initially met John Wayne Gacy. After all, the store was only a few short blocks from the roadcut construction site. Maybe Gacy befriended them at Mr. Burns' store and won their confidence and trust over ice cream, I wondered aloud. It was a chilling thought to think this harmless iconic place—a source of great childhood memories—could have been invaded by such a sinister presence imposing itself on the innocence of our pastoral town.

We drive on to the six hundred block of Union Street to see where the Dowell family home once sat directly behind the Hoag's place. Now only a parking lot covers the house's original footprint, but the vibrations and energy from a previous time remains in the neighborhood, Mary explains. "They were driving with Gacy in this area," she says.

I turn right onto Birch Street/Highway 79 and drive a few blocks south through the roadcut area where the ominous cave system was first exposed during the highway construction in the spring of 1967. Ironically, Mary also feels nothing related to the boys as we drive across the subterranean cave system below. For half a century, the conventional theory about the lost boys' fate had been settled; the trio was likely buried in a collapsed cave passage in the complicated maze cave network. But history was now quickly being rewritten with an astonishing twist.

Pointing to the left, I explain this was the last place the three lost boys had been seen at a quarter past five on May 10, 1967, standing up on the roadcut slope along the eastern edge of Highway 79.

"I see the boys coming from their house. I see Gacy up there too. He was watching," Mary says. She chillingly reminds me of her earlier channeling that showed Gacy was the mystery man seen for two or three days at the road construction site prior to the boys' disappearance. "Gacy was watching them. He had his eyes on the boys and a young highway construction worker." The highway construction worker, a very fortunate man, would escape fate's roulette.

A few hundred yards south, we make a left turn and take the steep and winding road up to Lovers Leap, the prominent geologic overlook offering spectacular views of the Hannibal area. The Rileys enjoy the view from the top as we are buffeted by a damp, chilly wind. Mary, her long blonde hair blowing in the breeze, looks around deep in thought, assessing the summit. "I feel the boys were here. I feel heavy and sad also. I think Gacy is toying with us." Mary walks to the safety fence bordering the edge of the cliff face, and suddenly her focus intensifies. She points her finger downward to flat land three hundred feet below, announcing with urgency, "I want to go down there!" I'm startled by the forcefulness of her request and take note that she has plugged into something from beyond as we head to the car.

What she did not know, what she could not know having never been to Hannibal, is that a narrow, little-used road overgrown by trees and brush runs north-south along the base of the Lovers' Leap bluff. It's Bluff Street, also traveled during the previous exploration tours with Cat and Britney. The former "River Road" once ran for several miles along the railroad tracks and nearby Mississippi River. Now, we will follow it for less than a mile before dead-ending at a gravel parking area on the river's western shore.

The psychics' intense interest in this stretch of road makes sense. Back in 1967, with State Highway 79 under construction, taking River Road would have been the fastest, most efficient way to quickly get out of town without being seen, I privately theorize. The southside neighborhood was teeming with children at the time, and this route would have ensured a quick getaway, minimizing any chance of being noticed.

We turn from Fulton Avenue onto Bluff Street and are immediately in the country with no signs of human life outside our vehicle. Both sides of the road are overgrown with trees and brush giving it a mysterious feel as we lumber down the narrow, deteriorating road alone, as if in an Alfred Hitchcock drama.

I had set the odometer to track our advance. The only sound is the quiet movement of air from the air conditioning vent. My digital audio record runs silently, ready to capture Mary's comments. Mary lowers her head, closes her eyes and breathes deeply as we slowly roll along.

At one-tenth of a mile, Mary grabs her stomach. "Oh boy," she says with concern. We continue our slow progress. At two-tenths of a mile down Bluff Street she utters, "I feel uneasy, sick to my stomach. I feel like Gacy is watching me. He has a lot of dark energy that is so draining," she says, looking distressed. At three-tenths of a mile, Mary firmly states, "I feel we're in an important area for this whole deal."

As the other two psychics had sensed during their visits in mid-August, Mary now senses this was the route out of town once Gacy had the three abducted boys captive in his car. "I keep seeing Gacy's car ahead of us. He's very upset. The right side of my face hurts, my ear is throbbing, and I hear a voice scream 'Stop it!' Someone was beaten."

When she pauses, just as we reach the turnaround point on the road, I stop the Land Rover and look at her. "This is incredible," I say. "All three of you have sensed the exact same situation, the same emotions, the same behavior, fifty-one years after the event, on this very stretch of road. Absolutely extraordinary."

Like the others, Mary sees Bluff Street as the location where Gacy's offer of a ride home for the three adventurous boys suddenly had gone terribly wrong. "I feel the boys, and I feel Gacy, and he's *very* upset and out of control," Mary says ominously.

Mary is now eager to explore Highway 79 on the other side of the Lovers' Leap bluff. "I feel drawn to go that way," she says, pointing southward. We double back and hop onto the highway, soon passing the turnoff to historic Mark Twain Cave, as we'd done twice before. Mary is focusing deeply as she looks at the lush green of the forested hills moving past the passenger window. We drive for a few minutes when her head snaps to the right looking at the woods just north of the Continental Cement Plant's entrance.

"Stop, I don't need to go any further," she says firmly. My eyes are wide as I ponder the significance of her statement. Incredibly, we are back at the very location—the Three Deer Site—the other two psychics also had identified during their independent tours earlier.

"I feel drawn into the trees," Mary says. I park the SUV in front of a closed gate spanning a white gravel road, with tufts of high grass growing among the limestone rocks. We walk about two hundred yards, curving left into the small meadow surrounded by trees and dense brush. It is the same isolated, hidden area, unseen from Highway 79. I restrain myself from telling Mary I'd already been here twice.

The woods, valleys and hills of northern Ralls County would normally be a peaceful retreat from a chaotic world. On this day, the pastoral silence is broken only by the light rain drumming the leaves of the canopy overhead. But a darkness hangs heavy over this portion of northeast Missouri, and Mary is clearly feeling it deeply.

"I just feel pulled that way," Mary says as she points westward into the dense woods. She, Tanner and I step around the poison ivy and walk across the soggy mat of wet leaves, rotting tree downfall and some old beer cans. We continue for about fifty feet and stop. Mary explains, as she had previously channeled, that a shallow grave, no more than three or four feet deep, was waiting here on that fateful May evening in 1967 just to the left of Gacy's car.

Mary Riley at the Three Deer Site where she believes the boys are buried.
Photo by John Wingate.

Her impressions come quickly. "I feel very drawn to this area. This is where I feel the boys' presence. Gacy pulled off the highway and drove up into this wooded area. He sexually assaulted the boys, first Craig, then Joel. I'm very sick to my stomach mainly because Gacy is trying to revisit this, but I've already seen it, so I don't want to again see what he did to the boys. I can see the tail lights of Gacy's car, and he is assaulting the boys, then strangling them. I feel like it's harder to breathe, and my chest is very heavy."

Mary walks about ten feet to the left of the car she's seeing in her mind. "Their bodies would only be this far away from the dirt lane. He took the boys' bodies and dumped them here in a grave and then buried them. You're not going to have to go hike miles to find them, they're right here. It was getting dark by the time they were buried. Gacy watched the sun go down, and then he left."

I'm standing in stunned silence when the laconic Tanner announces, "I found a shoe." Mary and I look up to see him holding a woman's sandal of recent vintage. In a moment of perverse humor, I respond, "I don't think it's Gacy's size."

Mary senses both an evil thrill and an uneasiness in John Wayne Gacy on that fateful evening of May 10, 1967. "I think he thought it was going to be easy. Three young boys and him being a grown man, he felt he was capable of more than what he was able to easily handle. It was not an easy thing for him. I feel like this was his biggest crime, his biggest act at one point. And I do feel like these were among his first kills. I don't know if these were his first, but I do feel these were among his very first kills." Until now, Gacy's first known kill was in 1972, five years in the future. And, as far as we know, he never killed three individuals in the same evening.

Mary pauses for a moment and continues sharing her thoughts. "Gacy was in this area before he brought the boys here. I feel like he pre-planned this for sure. This wasn't a spur-of-the-moment *I'm just going to turn off the road and go up here.* He visited the area previously, dug the grave and prepared for this."

We stand quietly as a light rain falls. A somber, funereal mood settles over us as we stare at the wet forest floor, not quite knowing what to do or say. "I feel a calm now from the boys," Mary says, breaking the silence. "They're okay now. Their spirit energy is peaceful in the spirit world. I feel like that's a sense of comfort they're sharing with me on this whole journey we've taken together. I'm wondering if they're giving me a sign... grateful somebody knows that they're here, and they're peaceful knowing that somebody is not going to stop looking for them."

After living with this tragedy for half a century, it was difficult to fathom another outcome, one so depraved and darkly evil, then, to literally stand where intuitive mediums all independently agreed the boys were tortured, murdered and buried. It was almost too much to handle. I wanted to drop to my knees and start digging.

Drone aerial photo of Three Deer Site in northern Ralls County, Missouri.

If these three psychics are correct, by the time it was dark on May 10, 1967 the three lost boys of Hannibal were dead and buried together in a shallow grave as the largest cave search in US history was just beginning to unfold two miles to the north. The search drama would become big news; a historic month-long, around-the-clock odyssey that would, in the end, reveal nothing about the boys' true fate.

I had experienced all of this with my own eyes. Throughout this investigation, I made sure all three psychics were "siloed," set apart from each other, so there would be no sharing of information. Only Cat and Mary knew each other through a family connection, but both had agreed not to compare notes. Britney knew neither of the other two women. Despite the remarkable accuracy of these three women, I still struggled with getting my mind around this strange new reality.

While I was in Hannibal, I figured it was a good time to reconnect with Britney to see if she had sensed anything more about this astonishing case. We talked over Greek salads at an eclectic restaurant, LaBinnah (Hannibal spelled backwards). While Britney was bringing me up to speed on her medium activities, her face suddenly darkened, and her focus strayed to somewhere beyond.

"Gacy just dropped in. That's how he always does... he drops in and leaves," she tells me. "He just had one word—congratulations."

"Congratulations? For what," I ask, leaning closer. "What do you think it means?" Britney looked me square in the eyes and dropped the bombshell. "It couldn't be any clearer. You've solved it."

Britney was completely unaware of my activities in Hannibal this day, but somehow the spirit of John Wayne Gacy knew what had been discovered.

Chapter 11
Stranger in Town

Reflecting on the extraordinary findings of the Hannibal investigation, we are left seeking the answer to an elusive key question. What possible reason did John Wayne Gacy have for being in Hannibal on May 10, 1967? What was it that caused his twisted life to intersect with the lives of the three light-hearted boys in childhood's full bloom? Did he have a specific purpose for being in town that fateful day? Was he just driving through on his way elsewhere?

During extensive research, I did discover an interesting Gacy connection to Hannibal, one that stems from the killer's artistic side. While on death row at Menard Penitentiary in Marion, Illinois, Gacy was producing scores of oil paintings. The paintings had a folk-art quality to them, some a bit crude... skulls comprised of nude bodies, likenesses of fellow criminals Ed Gein and Charles Manson; other works depicted Disney characters, landscapes, baseball themes; and his numerous self-portraits as a clown, in full makeup and colorful costume. There was even a painting of a thorn-crowned Jesus Christ.

The art was painted with a naïve style similar to that of an elementary or middle school student with a budding art talent. The amateurish brush strokes, gently applied to canvas, bely the terrible twisted mind of the artist. His psychiatrist, Helen Morrison, noticed in many of the landscapes the shadows were painted backward, opposite of how the sun would cast them. The style was just like Gacy the person, Morrison observed. "On first glance, the person seemed fine, nice, almost cheery. But peering at the inside, into the grim underbelly, he was all off-kilter."

Gacy painting of his character Pogo the Clown. Provided photo.

Gacy's creative avocation helped launch a lucrative murderabilia market for art lovers who desire the creative works of criminals and madmen. What would motivate someone to have such an interest? Serial killers wield a strange hold over a substantial sector of the general public; their horrendous crimes are seen as both appalling and fascinating. In many ways, serial killers are for adults what monster movies are for kids, equal parts scary and oddly mesmerizing to follow. Some individuals collect murderabilia for historical interest, while others have an interest in crime and its dark players. Other collectors enjoy owning something with a grim and macabre history. And still others step up and collect the dark creations to ensure they're unavailable and never seen again. After Gacy's execution, two Chicago area businessmen purchased more than ten thousand dollars worth of Gacy art and destroyed the paintings in a public—and very cathartic—bonfire.

Ironically, the small firm marketing the Gacy paintings was located in Hannibal and operated by two of the killer's nephews. "From about 1992 to 1994, Ray Kasper, one of Gacy's nephews, and Kasper's cousin Shawn Jackson operated Jac-Kas Productions in Hannibal," explained Jim Turantos, a former Illinois state investigator who now, in semi-retirement in Las Vegas, serves as the official executor for a website selling Gacy's art. (A portion of the proceeds goes to The National Center for Victims of Crime.)

In the early 1990s, Jackson lived in the twelve-hundred block of Fulton Avenue on Hannibal's southside, just blocks from the Hoag and Dowell families' homes. Jac-Kas Productions marketed Gacy's paintings by sending out more than 750 fliers advertising autographed paintings. And the demand for these creative works was strong. Among the sale items were variations of Disney's Seven Dwarfs theme for $150 apiece and a 16-by-20-inch clown painting for $199 or $235 if the buyer also wanted an autographed photo of Gacy included. A promotion also said the killer could be commissioned to paint an individual portrait for $200.

One of Gacy's customers was the official photographer for then-Illinois-Governor James Thompson. When Thompson discovered some of Gacy's paintings were being showcased as part of the Illinois State Fair's inmate art exhibit, he tried to stop the display but acted too late. All six of Gacy's paintings had quickly sold.

The men of Jac-Kas Productions were keen to profit from anything Gacy-related, and the sales proceeds were shared with the artist. Gacy used his profits to purchase art supplies, cigars, snacks and to fund his legal appeal, his fourth and final attempt to get his conviction overturned. Gacy also had substantial postage overhead due to being a pen-pal to nearly twenty thousand followers worldwide.

"Gacy eventually felt Jac-Kas Productions wasn't being fair with the money. He was disenchanted with the revenue and where it was going," Turantos explained. "Things quickly started going south in the relationship."

On October 5, 1993, Illinois Attorney General Roland Burris filed suit on behalf of the Illinois Department of Corrections to recover the art profits to cover some of the costs of housing the mass murderer on Death Row. The suit had a secondary goal of preventing Gacy from financially benefiting from the sale of his artwork. The Department of Corrections requires inmates who wish to operate a business to first secure approval, but Gacy had failed to obtain official permission. "There's nothing wrong with inmates painting. There's nothing wrong with them corresponding. But if they're doing business, they must have approval of the warden," said Corrections Department Spokesman Nic Howell at the time.

The lawsuit, filed in Randolph County, sought $141,000, the cost of Gacy's incarceration since July 1982. A Burris spokesman said the state believed the murderer was "reasonably able to pay" for his food and housing which cost $41.61 a day in the early 1990s.

A reporter for the *Chicago Tribune* contacted Jac-Kas Productions in 1993 and spoke to a man who responded defensively and refused to identify himself. "We understand there are some people out there who would consider this morally wrong," the man said. "But this is a country founded upon the free merchandising system. It's capitalism. We're not putting out TV commercials. We're not putting out huge newspaper ads. There are people out there who want to buy these things, and we want to sell them," the man explained.

It's not clear how much the state recovered from Gacy's art enterprise, the records are now unavailable, but most of the paintings were confiscated, and others remain available online, with most proceeds going to charity. After the lawsuit was concluded, Attorney General Burris and the Cook County State's Attorney Jack O'Malley asked the Illinois Supreme Court to set an execution date.

Turantos personally visited Gacy on May 6, 1994, just four days before his execution. "We made eye contact. He gave me a nod and shook my hand and invited me to sit down," Turanto recalled. "Gacy was very nice, with a cordial and professional demeanor. The prison guards left us alone and let him run the show."

During the visit, Turantos said he felt the strength of Gacy's personality. "He was a master manipulator who denied the murders and blamed them on a split in the mind. He was able to fit into society and had fooled a lot of people, but he had a yen for the dark side. It was John and Jack, and Jack was the killer," Turantos said. The meeting lasted for ninety minutes, then Gacy said he had a schedule to keep. Time had been slotted for the famous inmate's next visitor—television journalist Geraldo Rivera.

There is no evidence Gacy had family to visit in Hannibal back in the late 1960s. However, a long, lingering rumor has persisted all these many years since Gacy's arrest made him a household name. The rumor mill had efficiently spread the theory that Gacy was part of the State Highway 79 highway construction crew. This is untrue, as we now know that Gacy was living and working in Waterloo, Iowa, managing his father-in-law's three Kentucky Fried Chicken restaurants. But if Gacy had briefly been in Hannibal in May 1967, one can certainly imagine the masterful liar telling people he was part of the road crew to explain his presence in town.

Hannibal police were usually aware of these kinds of rumors, burning like a lit fuse through the small town. Gossip traveled fast across backyard fences here. When the lost boys' rumor emerged after the Gacy arrest made headlines, the police chief took action to find some answers.

In a police department memo dated February 22, 1979, two months and a day after Gacy's Chicago arrest, Police Chief Franklin Neff notified the Detective Division about a stunning lead that had failed to get prompt attention. In the memo entitled *Investigation of John Gacy,* Neff wrote to the Detective Division's Captain Ronald L. Long:

> On or about January 12, 79, Oney Kirby 221-XX67 reported he had heard Gacy, involved in some 28 [sic] murders, was in Hannibal possibly as a bartender on [the] Southside during the time of the three lost boys in the caves. At that time, I gave it to Capt. Webster, today I learn Mr. Kirby has never been contacted or any investigation made. Please contact Kirby, apologize for the inattention we have given him and assign someone to it. Keep me advised. Chief Neff.

The task was assigned to Lieutenant Kenneth L. Caldwell who presented a detailed supplementary report on April 28, 1979. Captain Long had requested the rumor be "checked discreetly" that Gacy "may have worked at a tavern located on Fulton Ave. near Terrace Avenue." Caldwell took some time with his investigation. His final report detailed a history of southside Hannibal taverns that seemed to frequently change names with each new ownership. It concluded:

> The officer has attempted to contact [name] several times to follow-up on the information of the tavern in the 1000 block of Fulton Ave. but has not been able to make contact with him. During officer's investigation, the name Gacy was not mentioned by [the] officer or any of the persons interviewed. From officer's information gathered up until now, the tavern probably was operated about 1959 or 1960 and would not have been in operation during the time that the Hoag [and Dowell] boys were lost in the Murphy caves. From previous [citizen] information, Gacy may have been a bartender at this tavern during the Murphy Cave incident, but apparently this tavern would have not been in business during this time.

Hannibal resident Oney Kirby died in 2007 at the age of ninety-one, so there is no additional information about the source of the rumor he heard and passed along to police.

Police Chief Neff wasn't giving up on the inquiry despite the dead end on the Kirby lead. Government documents from the period reveal a paper trail between Hannibal Police and the Federal Bureau of Investigation. On June 26, 1979, Chief Neff instructed Detective Captain Long to write FBI Special Agent Jeffrey Moss:

On May 10, 1967, three young Hannibal boys disappeared, presumably lost in one of the numerous caves on the south side of Hannibal. There was never any definite evidence that they were in the caves, and an extensive search failed to reveal the bodies.

Needless to say, there have been many stories, guesses and rumors that they ran away from home, were possibly kidnapped and so forth. Also, the family and the Police Department have received many tips and leads from all over the country as to their whereabouts, and even from ESP experts, all of which we have attempted to follow through.

We would like to ask your assistance in checking out one such lead. The Hannibal Police received information in January of 1979 that John Gacy, arrested for murder of a number of young boys, was living in Hannibal in 1967 and worked as a bartender. He was recognized during a television broadcast on the Gacy murders.

Will you please look into this matter, and if possible, ascertain if Gacy reports or states he lived in Hannibal during the 1960s?

The boys are: Joel Wise Hoag, 13, 5-6, 120 lbs., brown hair, medium build; William Francis Hoag, 12 (sic), 5-10, 86 lbs, red hair, blue eyes; Edwin Craig Dowell, 14, 5-10, 155 lbs, medium build, light brown curly hair, blue eyes.

Naturally at this time we are keeping this extremely confidential, with only the Chief of Police and myself knowing of this letter, in order to avoid burdening the parents unnecessarily.

We will most sincerely appreciate any information or assistance you may be able to give us in this matter.

Very truly yours,

J. Franklin Neff, Chief of Police

By: Ronald L. Long, Captain, Detective Division

On January 28, 1980, Hannibal Police Chief J. Franklin Neff received a response from FBI Special Agent in Charge Roy B. Klager, Jr.:

Dear Chief Neff:

Reference is made to your previous request for investigative assistance by the Federal Bureau of Investigation in determining the whereabouts of John Wayne Gacy during 1967, with regard to his possible involvement in an investigation initiated in 1967 by the Hannibal Police Department. Through contact with the Des Plaines, Illinois, Police Department it was determined that previous investigation conducted by that department indicated that Gacy had assisted his father-in-law in the operation of several Kentucky Fried Chicken restaurants in the Waterloo, Iowa area during 1966 and 1967, at which time Gacy's mother resided in Little Rock, Arkansas. Information was also provided that Gacy was believed to have been previously affiliated with the Jaycees in Springfield, Illinois, in 1964 and, following his move to Waterloo, Iowa, in 1966, he was involved in some type of trouble in Waterloo, Iowa, in 1967, which carried over to 1968.

Through subsequent investigation conducted by the Springfield Division of the Federal Bureau of

173

Investigation, Gacy's father-in-law, Fred Myers Jr. was located and interviewed in Springfield, Illinois, on December 3, 1979, at which time he recalled that Gacy had been previously employed at the Roberts Brothers Clothing Store in Springfield, Illinois, until around 1966, at which time Gacy moved to Waterloo, Iowa, where he assisted Myers in the operation of three Kentucky Fried Chicken restaurants for the next several years. Myers further advised that, to his knowledge, Gacy never resided or was employed in Hannibal, Missouri, at any time in the past.

I trust that the above information will be of benefit to your department in connection with this investigative matter, and it is indeed a pleasure to have had the opportunity to assist your department in this regard.

Very truly yours,

Roy B. Klager, Jr.

Special Agent in Charge

While the evidence was clear Gacy did not ever live or work in Hannibal, the letter from FBI Agent Klager did offer a tantalizing tidbit that points to a plausible reason Gacy could have been in Hannibal during May 1967. He mentioned that Gacy's mother, Marion, was living with her younger daughter, Karen, in Little Rock, Arkansas, at that time.

In August of 1979, an interdepartmental memo between two FBI Special Agents referenced information from the Des Plaines Police Department about Gacy's possible travels during the spring of 1967:

[The detective] stated that it is possible that Gacy passed through Hannibal while en route to Little Rock, Arkansas, to visit his mother, but stated that such a stop would have been for less than two weeks.

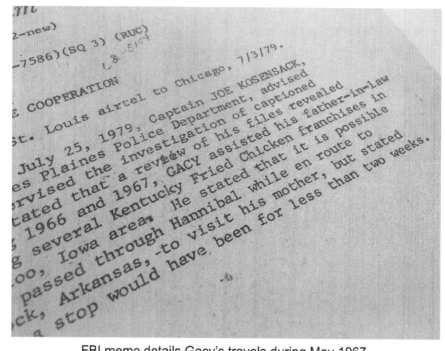

FBI memo details Gacy's travels during May 1967.

Finally, a credible rationale for Gacy's presence in Hannibal when the boys went missing. In a January 10, 1979 story in the *New York Times*, Gacy's younger sister, Karen, described her brother as someone who could never do enough for the family. She said he kept in touch with frequent telephone calls and always visited them once or twice a year in Little Rock.

Living in Waterloo, if Gacy drove to Little Rock to see his mother and sister, his route took him south on State Highway 61 which cuts across the western boundary of Hannibal. If he had desired a more scenic route, he would have cut through town and taken State Highway 79, a hilly drive with beautiful views of the Mississippi River and the high Lincoln Hills. But had he done so in May 1967, he would have been stopped by the Highway 79 construction underway.

One can easily imagine Gacy approaching the huge construction area and seeing the southside neighborhood teeming with young boys and girls, the early progeny of the post-World War II Baby Boom. While it is speculative to ponder, one can imagine Gacy deciding to stay a day or two and check out the neighborhood and its plentiful potential victims, full of trust and innocence borne of small-town living. He may have felt a dark, murderous obsession welling up inside him, demanding to be fed and satisfied quickly.

Significantly, we must remember that May 14, 1967, just four days after the lost boys disappeared, was Mother's Day. And Gacy never missed celebrating the day with his beloved mother. Little Rock was a nearly direct seven-hour drive from Hannibal.

I believe it is highly likely John Wayne Gacy was the mystery man seen at the highway roadcut site for two days before the boys went missing, as witnessed by the construction workers in 1967, and psychically sensed in great detail by Britney Buckwalter and Mary Riley fifty-one years later in 2018.

Chapter 12
A Most Unusual Police Visit

After Mary Riley and I had completed our tour of the Hannibal area, she met later that day with Denise Hoag-Mudd, Joel and Billy's younger sister, to share the amazing details of our tour and findings. Denise phoned a friend who is a Ralls County Deputy Sheriff to make an appointment to discuss the astonishing findings. "I'm five minutes away... I'll just stop by," the officer reportedly said.

After they briefed the officer on the events of the summer, he asked Mary to follow him to the Ralls County Sheriff's Department on the edge of town to make a formal statement. "I spoke with another officer at the sheriff's office, and I could tell he was pretty skeptical. He had never really dealt with a medium, and he didn't know what to think of me," Mary said.

"He had a lot of questions about how this all works and how it came about. When we had concluded our discussion, he said, 'Okay, this is pretty crazy,'" Mary added. "I have people coming in confessing to crimes all the time, and they provide less detail than what you've provided here tonight," the officer reportedly said, astonished by the situation.

Then, as if to test her abilities, officers asked Mary to visit another location to channel a recent homicide case. Details are not available as Mary signed a confidentiality agreement not to divulge evidence in the open case, but she clearly made a strong impression. "After I told them what I saw, they felt I was legitimate and gave me one of those, *Who is this lady?* looks."

By the time Mary left the Ralls County Sheriff's Department it was ten thirty. It had been a very long and intense day, a historic day during her first visit to Mark Twain's boyhood hometown.

To ponder these lost boys falling at the hands of a monstrous madman pains the heart. We will only know with certainty when authorities dig where directed by our psychic sleuths.

Steve Sederwall, who grew up in Hannibal and was friends with Craig Dowell, is a former Los Angeles Police Department officer with a sixth sense for details in a case. Now semi-retired, he operates Cold West Detective Agency near Capitan, New Mexico. While Sederwall is now typically solving crimes from the Wild West days, he found the information revealed in this book extraordinary and impossible to ignore.

"As cops, we're trained to follow the evidence. So, we can't depend solely on what psychics report, but given the corroboration among these three women, you would do the case a huge disservice to ignore it," Sederwall said. "I don't think you can discount this information. Out of the whole world, these three women identified the same locations. What's next? You go look for the bodies."

We have the GPS coordinates where these women believe the remains rest—the wooded Three Deer Site west of State Highway 79, a few miles south of Lovers Leap. I have provided these global positioning coordinates to the Ralls County Sheriff's Department and Hannibal Police.

The lost boys' incident remains an open case with the Hannibal Police Department. On a spring day, I spoke with Assistant Police Chief John Zerbonia and revealed the fruits of the months-long investigation. He was quiet, listening carefully at the astonishing story being conveyed on the call. I inquired whether authorities might utilize cadaver dogs, ground penetrating radar and/or conduct limited digging at the identified location. We must try to locate a crude grave that is believed to contain the bones of three children who deserve a better final resting place, I explained.

Zerbonia said in a situation such as this, the police department would likely rely on the Missouri State Highway Patrol or the Federal Bureau of Investigations' Forensics Team. "They're trained to conduct a dig to ensure the chain of evidence in the case," he explained. He made a point of recommending that individuals such as myself not conduct the digging on their own, due to the possible presence of important evidence that remains in any grave. "I have no plans to go rogue on this and conduct a dig on my own," I reassured him.

Zerbonia said he would discuss the matter with Police Chief Lyndell Davis. For now, the next move is for local law enforcement to decide how to proceed. There is no real urgency, of course. The three boys and John Wayne Gacy are deceased, and Hannibal police have plenty of other criminal cases to occupy them. For now, we must wait. But circumstances demand further police inquiry into what has been revealed.

This matter of digging is a complicated affair. Paranormal sensing by the most experienced mediums is an imprecise endeavor to a certain extent; it relies on the abilities of the mediums to accurately understand and interpret the often abstract information they are tapping into from across the preternatural divide. The boys' bodies may be buried at the precise Ralls County location identified by the psychics, or 30 feet or 150 feet or farther from the sensed burial location. We have an identified location to begin digging, but if remains are not found at that very spot, how far would authorities extend any digging? And at what point would the digging be halted on private property?

We are tantalizingly close to knowing the outcome of this remarkable paranormal odyssey. From this point, we leave this investigation in the hands of law enforcement to report on any future activities that may bring this mystery to a final resolution. For now, the unsettling mystery remains with us, as family members, friends and so many others await hopeful news that will bring the boys to their final resting places.

When we lose a beloved family member or friend, the grieving is hard. As the saying goes, grief is the price you pay for love. At birth, we welcome a child into our world to love, nurture and guide. They burst into our reality brimming with potential, and we find such joy in their presence. We teach them to read, ride a bike, do well in school, grow in their faith and learn to be a friend and responsible citizen. We find great meaning in our children. In fact, we grow and learn as much as they do in our time together.

Every day is a gift to be treasured and used well, but Joel, Billy and Craig, their promises and destinies aborted, succumbed to a terrible childhood fate. Never would they know the joys that remained out of reach—the miracle of that first cry at birth, as the swaddled newborn child is drawn close to the heart. Never would they know the feeling of starting a family, becoming accomplished at a skill and using their gifts to do good things. Never would they grow into and through the blessings of middle age and the autumn of life.

Lives dreadfully cut short. So many people have lived this reality for more than half a century. We lost sons, brothers, uncles and friends—these Sons of Hannibal—who were so full of life and barely midway to manhood.

Until there is full resolution to this remarkable odyssey, we reflect on what has been revealed in a most incredible manner, from a place beyond the boundaries of our material world. We thank the dedicated women—Mary, Britney and Cat—who so bravely shared what they have seen despite their reluctance to seek public attention.

One fall evening after exchanging text messages with Mary Riley, I went outdoors to the patio back home in Minnesota. It was a crisp night, and a clear sky twinkled overhead. The blazing firepit was a source of warmth, comfort and quiet reflection. Sitting there, I was swept up by a wave of wonder as I gazed up at the bright, celestial tapestry spreading infinitely across the heavens. I was struck by the irony that this was the same sky a madman had seen after completing his twisted and perverted pleasures, borne in supernatural darkness inside that depraved mind.

Two very different moments, but one truth remains—love, in all its forms, is stronger than evil. The grief felt by family and friends for the lost three boys, even now, reflects the lasting affections that still burn in hearts across America.

This story found me; I did not search it out. In fact, I was conducting research for another book when these developments came to light. I struggled for a few weeks about whether this book should be written and shared. There were many three in the morning awakenings as my active mind considered this bizarre reality. I had many discussions with my wife and a pastor friend who counseled that while the supernatural realm is unknowable and should be avoided, perhaps God *was* doing something remarkable through the participants in this amazing and mysterious preternatural pilgrimage across time. I came away certain the story would be a fascinating study of the paranormal events through the lens of the Christian worldview.

I finally decided to write *Souls Speak* after Britney Buckwalter shared what she heard from Craig Dowell during another channeling session. "I have to tell you something. Craig just said, 'Thank you, John, for giving us a voice.'"

My eyes clouded in this astonishing moment as I pondered the words.

Even after all of the remarkable experiences witnessed during the summer and fall of 2018, I remain flabbergasted by these abilities. Beyond space and time, in that mysterious realm of vibration and eternal spiritual energy, spirit elements already knew this story would be written. I cautiously took this as a sign of encouragement; I would proceed carefully to honor old friends gone too soon. There was no other choice—I simply could not let them down.

Postscript

More Unsettling Mystery

Just before Christmas 2018, as I was writing the manuscript for *Souls Speak*, I called Mary Riley in rural Wyoming to see if she had sensed anything new in the Hannibal case. She was in good spirits, enjoying the holidays with Tanner and the kids at the family homestead as fresh snowfall blanketed the western landscape. She had not channeled anything more from John Gacy. However, she did acknowledge sensing new energies she believes may be the spirits of additional victims. "Normally when I connect with spirit, I can channel or communicate with it. But not these," Mary said. "It may be that these are the spirits of younger children who don't fully understand who I am and how this works."

Mary said the number three was shown her. Could this represent three more victims in the area? "It may," she said. "I also picked up the word *Louisiana* which may mean the town south of Hannibal."

John Wayne Gacy likely made the drive to Little Rock, Arkansas many times. If he traveled State Highway 79 to the St. Louis area, his route took him through Louisiana, Missouri. Are there other unidentified victims there or elsewhere along the route still to be discovered?

It is difficult to believe Gacy's evil pathological nature only emerged in Chicago between the years 1972 and 1978, a schedule of killings tidily bookended by the calendar. Based upon his psychiatric profile, he was quite possibly killing regularly on drives from Waterloo to Little Rock and earlier when he lived in Springfield, Illinois and briefly in Las Vegas, Nevada after high school. How could he not?

A man I'll identify as BG because he wishes anonymity, related an incident that happened to him in Springfield, Illinois when he was a teenager in the 1960s. "I remember a guy stopped me as I was walking through a car dealership parking lot and asked me if I wanted to smoke some weed. He creeped me out because he was older, and I'd never had an adult ask me something like that before," BG said.

"I had a couple of choice words for him, and he got pissed, gassed the car and drove off. I remember the car. It was a dark-colored four-door sedan, what we called a land barge back then."

This sounds like the car described by Mary Riley and Britany Buckwalter.

Years later, after BG realized Gacy had once lived in Springfield, he conducted his own research. "I discovered he had lived at 3309 Normandy. That's about three blocks from the car dealership where this incident happened. I bring this up because police should look into missing boys in the Springfield area during that era."

Rafael Tovar was a Des Plaines, Illinois police officer who assisted with the Gacy investigation in 1978. Tovar's last conversation with Gacy reportedly occurred while he was transferring the killer from the Des Plaines police station to a Cook County facility in Chicago.

During the drive, Tovar reportedly asked Gacy, "John, we've been running around, and I don't want to be running around forever. How many bodies are we looking for?"

Gacy was coy, "Well, you know, I told my lawyers there's about thirty, thirty some odd. You know what? The number forty-five sounds really good."

"Really?" Tovar replied.

"Yeah, sounds really good," said Gacy.

"Well, where are the rest of them?" Tovar asked.

"That's for you to find out," came the reply.

Former Gacy prosecutor Terry Sullivan called Gacy the "worst of all murderers." He stated, "There's no reason to believe Gacy didn't kill one hundred people. We knew there were thirty-three, but in my mind, I'm pretty certain he had other victims."

The Des Plaines, Illinois Police Lieutenant Joseph Kozenczak, who tirelessly led the 1978 Gacy investigation, took Gacy at his word when the killer scribbled across the back of his painting of an Arkansas farmhouse, *Find the bodies if you can.* "I am convinced Gacy killed a lot more than thirty-three people," Kozenczak stated.

William Dorsch, a tactical officer with the Chicago Police in the 1970s, lived on West Miami Avenue in a quiet working-class neighborhood near O'Hare Airport. Gacy's mother Marion lived in a nearby apartment building during that time, and Gacy was frequently there doing odd jobs for her. Dorsch knew Gacy and thought nothing of encountering him late at night, as Gacy was known to keep odd hours.

In the summer of 1975, Dorsch was wrapping up a very long day as he returned home at three in the morning. As he turned onto a side street near his home, he saw a husky man, short of stature, crossing the street carrying a shovel. As Dorsch got closer, he recognized it was Gacy.

"John, it's three o'clock in the morning. What are you doing?" Dorsch asked.

Gacy responded with a laugh, "Bill, you know me, not enough hours in the day. You get it done when you can."

Years later, after Gacy's execution, word of the Miami Avenue incident found its way to the Better Government Association (BGA) in Chicago, a watchdog group. In November of 1998, the BGA funded a ground-penetrating radar scan of the apartment property where Marion Gacy had once lived. The radar survey identified two suspicious areas in the frozen earth, and Chicago Police began to dig. A large crowd of onlookers and media crews surrounded the property anxiously awaiting dramatic news. But the dig ended unceremoniously. The only items found were a glass marble, a damaged saucepan, a chunk of concrete and a length of wire, but no human remains were located—at least in the small area where they dug.

Cook County Detective Sergeant Jason Moran, who has successfully identified many Gacy victims, continues his work to identify six remaining victims from the 1970s Chicago murder spree. In a phone conversation, Moran told me there is no known evidence at this time to tie Gacy to any other murders. "His known victims were all killed in the residence," he said.

While acknowledging there's no new official evidence to link Gacy to additional victims, he doesn't rule out the possibility. "It's hard to put it past someone so evil," Moran said to a *Chicago Tribune* reporter. "Gacy was a traveler. He'd travel all over the country for business and pleasure. How did he turn it off [the urge to kill]?"

Moran explained Gacy's gift for setting a trap for naïve victims. "He would build up trust with his victims so they wouldn't need to be on guard," he explained. "He was their employer, their friend." Police say Gacy would frequently provide food, alcohol or drugs to win someone's trust and confidence. "That's an easy way to kill someone," Moran told the *Chicago Tribune* in December 2018, the fortieth anniversary of Gacy's arrest.

It was a dark formula for getting close to children and young adults in big cities and small towns.

Psychiatrist Dr. Helen Morrison did not consider Gacy a full-blown psychopath. Someone with a psychopathic personality type is able to "control what they do, think and feel," she wrote after the trial. Gacy, on the other hand, was a complete slave to his dark feelings, erupting suddenly with great fury to torture and kill, fully incapable of controlling himself.

She illustrated this point in her book, *My Life Among the Serial Killers*, with portions of a letter she had received from Gacy while he was incarcerated at Menard Penitentiary in southern Illinois. While on death row, Gacy was known as Boss Hogg, a corrupt and brash character from the popular television show of the era, *Dukes of Hazzard*. Like the character, Gacy was portly and smoked cigars. His fellow inmates, however, didn't always appreciate his bravado and bold nature. In the letter to Doctor Morrison, Gacy wrote:

> Last week I came on one guy in the library who wanted me to go into the back room to talk with him with four more backing him up. Now, I informed the captain... that I had been threatened by this individual, but they just say to go in and kick his ass... While I am not afraid of him, I am afraid of myself. I don't believe in fighting, never have, but if I have to set an example, then someone will get killed. I told [the guy] which side of me does he want to talk to, and which side of me does he want to fight with. He didn't answer, just walked away. But sooner or later that's not going to work. I am afraid I am going to hurt someone. Because once it starts, I will have no control over it.

Gacy was a psychologically incomplete human being who was able to play roles and maintain decorum, but only for a short time. Deep within his core, Gacy suffered from a cocktail of mental psychoses, including a multiple personality disorder. Addicted to killing, Gacy was fully unable to control the actions of his dark alter ego Bad Jack. There is no dispute on this point.

New Mexico cold case investigator and Hannibal native Steve Sederwall suspects Gacy was killing elsewhere during and before his murder spree in suburban Chicago. "We know that as a teenager Gacy was already developing a mindset for killing. He was thinking it through. He was threatening to drown kids when he was fifteen years old. That's far from normal."

"If he killed the Hannibal boys, they weren't likely his first victims," the seasoned cop speculated. "To kill three people, you have to be comfortable with killing and handling the bodies. He most likely had some kills before Hannibal. That's my guess. I'd suggest someone investigate missing persons and reports of bodies found in Waterloo, Springfield, Las Vegas, Missouri and Arkansas during the periods Gacy lived there, was visiting or driving through those areas."

It's been a long time since Sederwall last saw his buddy Craig Dowell racing up to his locker after school on Wednesday afternoon, May 10, 1967. Now, after fifty-two years, he prays for final closure in this haunting and devastating mystery, for the Hoags, the Dowells, their friends and for the other families who fell under the evil sway of John Wayne Gacy.

Did he kill beyond Chicago? Recall the numbers Mary Riley had seen during her first paranormal channeling session: 45-33-3-9. As you will recall from earlier in the book, we interpreted these numbers in this way:

> 45 was the number of victims Gacy mentioned to officer Tovar in 1978.

33 is the number of Chicago area victims.

3 represents the three Hannibal boys, for a total of 36 victims.

Subtract 36 from 45 and you get nine.

If we have interpreted these numbers correctly, based on what Mary Riley sensed, Gacy was killing consistently. Perhaps there are nine more murders not yet associated with him, nine more graves still to be discovered—somewhere.

Rickey Lee Enoch, missing from Monroe City, Missouri since June 30, 1977.

As an example, let's consider the suspicious and little-known disappearance case involving Rickey Lee Enochs. The eighteen-year-old blue-eyed blond teen went missing from Monroe City, Missouri, fifteen miles west of Hannibal, the afternoon of June 30, 1977. Family members indicate Rickey left his father's house with an unknown individual driving a vehicle with Illinois license plates. The teenager did not take any personal belongings with him and told his father he would return "in a little bit." Rickey Enochs has not been seen or heard from since. This incident sounds strangely familiar to the Robert Piest disappearance from the pharmacy where he was employed, Gacy's last kill before his arrest in December 1978.

John Wayne Gacy was still a free man in 1977 and continuing to kill. In fact, during 1977 Gacy killed at least nine of his Cook County, Illinois victims. And, of course, he drove a car with Illinois plates at the time. Had he come through Monroe City, perhaps offered Rickey Enochs a job and picked him up to discuss it further?

When I shared Rickey Enochs' photo with psychic Mary Riley, she came back with an unexpected and stunning response. "I say you found something! I have seen this boy several times before, and the connections are just crazy!

"Gacy hasn't come through for me directly yet, but Rickey showed me an image of John Wayne Gacy, and I saw the number nine yet again. Rickey got into his 'land barge-type car' like he was an acquaintance, like they'd had another meeting place previously. I believe Rickey Enochs is one of the nine previously unknown victims."

This seemed unbelievable, reminding me of the perfect fishing spot where you catch fish no matter where a line is dropped. I'd routinely sent Rickey's photo to Mary one evening and instantly got a hit. More puzzle pieces were, perhaps, revealing a scenario even larger than we had even imagined after the experience with the Hoag and Dowell boys.

Mary continued sharing what she had sensed from the unseen realm. "I feel an emptiness from Rickey Enochs, that he was forgotten as people stopped looking for him. It was like he just faded away. The feeling I get is that Gacy was acting like a mastermind, feeling above everyone else like he was the best. I think Gacy was using someone else's car for this one," Mary explained. By 1977, Gacy certainly had perfected the killing of young men and boys to a perverse art form and exuded confidence with his abilities to win people's confidence before they became his prey.

Regina 'Gina' Webb-Bradshaw is an FBI-trained cold case investigator who lives in central Missouri, a two-hour drive from Hannibal. She has served as a sheriff's deputy for several Missouri departments and spent a decade as special investigator for the Marion County Sheriff's Department, which has Hannibal and a portion of Monroe City in its jurisdiction. Highly respected by her colleagues, Bradshaw is unrelenting in her pursuit of a case, officers say.

When I shared highlights of this book with Bradshaw, she quickly acknowledged she has held similar suspicions about Gacy for many years. "It's a real possibility [he killed those Hannibal boys]. Gacy was living in Iowa, and his mother was in Little Rock. He would have driven Highway 61 straight through Hannibal," she said. Bradshaw believes it's highly improbable that Gacy limited his killing only to the years 1972 to 1978 in suburban Chicago. "We know he was victimizing people from an early age. As his sickness grew, his behavior worsened. He had a long, ongoing murder spree and was secure and sure of his craft," she said.

"I also can't see Gacy having only thirty-three victims, most of whom were underage. Studies show that a pedophile will typically have one hundred victims during their lifetime," said the seasoned sleuth who had spent years investigating sex and child crimes for the Carter County, Missouri prosecutor's office.

Parenthetically, the cold case investigator pointed out that over the decades Marion County, Missouri has seen a considerable number of missing persons per capita, something she partially attributes to the presence of the Mississippi River, a major north-south state Highway 61, and what she described as the dark and deep presence of a more than century-old criminal ring of "gypsy asphalters."

These laborers, Bradshaw said, prey on the public with driveway asphalt scams and many other cons. And they apparently enjoy a long legacy. "Mark Twain wrote a story in 1870 about the lightning rod salesman. That was the common gypsy scam during his lifetime. It goes that far back," Bradshaw explained. In Twain's story, his character is interrupted by an annoying and persistent door-to-door solicitor who sells him a veritable forest of lightning rods for his house.

According to Bradshaw, early in the twentieth century, immigrant labor from eastern Europe came to the Hannibal area to work at the new cement plant, which remains in operation in nearby Ralls County. "One of these gypsies told me that some of the wives back then worked as domestic servants for Hannibal's wealthy families. Over time, resentments developed, and some families started targeting the wealthy with scams," Bradshaw explained.

This gypsy justice has endured and evolved over the decades, remaining a strong criminal presence not only in Hannibal but in communities coast-to-coast.

Bradshaw says these perpetrators follow an old Gypsy Creed, always manipulating innocent people, even teaching their children to lie and scheme from a young age. "I've heard prison phone calls where these people were alerting family members to police interest or instructing them to destroy possible evidence."

This multi-generational criminal culture even has its own lingo. A *Mush* is a hired-hand or lower-level worker who does physical labor. A *Kite* is a person with no criminal history who will cash checks for the gypsy asphalters to maintain separation from the criminals and avoid a paper trail. Police are called *Muskers*, and federal agents are *Boya Muskers* or big cops.

"Everybody [associated with these gypsy asphalters] has got an angle, and everybody is trying to survive," said another source who wishes to remain anonymous. "I can tell you this... there is a sinister, criminal force in that area that terrifies many people."

Bradshaw says these con artists will travel to areas where road construction activity is underway and offer nearby homeowners "leftover asphalt" at a reduced price. Naïve homeowners quickly discover they've become unrelenting prey. An elderly Marion County Missouri woman was pressured to install seven lightning rods on her home and another four on a shed in a low-lying area not prone to lightning strikes. The installers typically place a colored ball on one lightning rod which alerts other con artists the homeowner is easy prey.

In the case of our elderly homeowner in Marion County, they continued to scam her with driveway asphalting and tree-trimming jobs that bilked her out of thousands of dollars. Then, adding insult to injury, the same persuasive and intimidating con artists sold her home health care services at a highly inflated price. "There is no end to what 'gypsy asphalters' are capable of," Bradshaw explained. "They steal, scam, sell drugs, even murder. There's no end to it."

The FBI-trained Bradshaw is currently investigating the September 13, 1999 disappearance of James Dale Yarbrough, a Palmyra resident who reportedly worked for a gypsy asphalting crew at an Iowa job site. The family man came home early from the job location and seemed fine, according to family members. He was home for a week or two and then vanished one morning between nine thirty and noon. Bradshaw says neither Yarbrough's bank account nor social security number were used after he went missing.

The experienced investigator suspects Yarbrough either saw or heard something he wasn't supposed to witness and was murdered to silence him. She holds this suspicion because, over time, the gypsy asphalters have grown less centralized with more criminal family rings that have expanded their criminal activity to include narcotics trafficking, she says.

"They tend to pursue their criminal activities outside the communities where they live," Bradshaw explained. "I've had calls from all over the US from law enforcement agencies inquiring about four Hannibal gypsy asphalter families in particular."

Bradshaw continues her investigation, and the Yarbrough disappearance remains an open case with the Marion County Sheriff's Department.

Another high-profile missing person case Bradshaw is investigating is that of Christina Whittaker. The twenty-one-year-old Hannibal woman, who suffered from a bipolar disorder, went missing November 13, 2009. Whittaker had become drunk and disorderly while enjoying too many drinks at Rookies Sports Bar. The brown-eyed redhead was asked to leave after she grew unruly with patrons. Whittaker asked several people for a ride home, but no one offered. Her cell phone was later found near her parked car.

You may recall from earlier in the book when psychic Britney Buckwalter focused on this missing person case. She clairvoyantly saw Whittaker accepting a ride from a black man who drove her to a party on Hannibal's southside. While at the party house, Buckwalter reported Whittaker apparently witnessed something she should not have seen, perhaps a drug deal or drug use. A man tells Whittaker's escort to "Get rid of her." Britney then psychically saw Christina being sexually assaulted near water and killed. Whittaker's family believes Christina was human trafficked in the Peoria, Illinois area.

The Whittaker case also remains open and unsolved at the Hannibal Police Department.

Last year, a New York-based documentary team, which continues to investigate the Whittaker case at this writing, received a jailhouse tip and brought two highly-trained cadaver dogs on separate days to a location along Warren Barrett Drive on Hannibal's western edge. "Each cadaver dog responds differently when they discover a burial site," Bradshaw explained. "Some paw at the dirt while others bark or jump. Both of these dogs independently reacted positively at the suspected burial location."

The documentary team quickly began to dig at the site, which is located on private property near Mills Creek, about one mile east of Highway 61. After digging several inches, they discovered what appeared to be a wire garrote (possibly for strangulation) and wire bindings. But before they could dig any deeper, men riding all-terrain-vehicles arrived and ordered the team to leave the property, even though the team had secured permission from the cooperative landowner to conduct the dig. Interestingly, Bradshaw told me a gypsy asphalter owns land nearby.

Bradshaw felt the unearthed artifacts significantly advanced the case and suspected the team had possibly located the spot where Whittaker's body, or another body, is buried. The evidence found at the scene was turned over to Hannibal Police.

Bradshaw suspects several families associated with the gypsy asphalter enterprises may be connected with or know something about Whittaker's and Yarbrough's fates or other missing persons cases. "There are several individuals in the area we know have specific information about Yarbrough. We know that. And I think our greatest hope for them is that someone steps up and takes accountability and responsibility and gives these families some closure."

As of this writing, the Whittaker and Yarbrough cases remain open and unsolved. These are two more examples of the many twists and turns involving missing persons in northeast Missouri.

Finally, this: In April 2019, I had a series of phone calls and emails with medium Mary Riley. She had channeled Gacy again and said, "He came through right away."

"The number nine came up again, and I'm confident there are nine more victims to be discovered," Mary said. "He also walked me through the Hannibal boys' deaths again and showed me the boys in the location we earlier visited (Three Deer Site) south of Hannibal." Mary said Gacy seemed more relaxed, calm and collected, and less cocky this time than he was initially. "He showed me a park on the edge of a small town, with a metal flag and some old swings with wooden seats," Mary explained. "He also showed me the name Jason and a wall covered with photos of missing persons." I tell her this information could refer to Jason Moran, the Cook County Detective who is tasked with identifying the final six unidentified Gacy victims in Chicago.

"I also see the initials J and W, and these have come up before when I've channeled Gacy," Mary explained. I search my memory, suddenly recalling the disappearance of a sixteen-year-old boy, John Wagner, also from Monroe City, Missouri, located near Hannibal. Wagner had vanished on February 17, 1968, nine months after the three Hannibal boys disappeared.

Coincidentally, the John Wagner disappearance is another case being pursued by cold case investigator Regina Bradshaw.

After dropping his brother off at a school dance, Bradshaw tells me that Wagner drove to an ice cream shop in the small downtown area, likely one of the few hangouts for teens on a Saturday night. While there, Wagner was involved in an altercation with Richard Eugene "Dickie" Dowell, twenty-two, apparently over Dowell's girlfriend showing an interest in Wagner.

"Dowell was known by police as a hothead, quick to anger and always ready to fight anyone," Bradshaw said.

John Wagner, missing from Monroe City, Missouri since February 17, 1968.

During the struggle, Wagner reportedly fell backward and struck his head on the sidewalk. In a panic, Dowell and two other older teens allegedly put Wagner in a car and drove off. The next morning, Wagner's truck, keys, coat and gloves were found in the alley off Main Street across from Dowell's Garage, an automotive repair business operated by Dickie Dowell's family. The Wagner boy's body has never been found.

Over the years, several individuals in the area have been questioned, and two persons of interest were administered polygraph tests, but the results were never publicly announced, and no one has been charged in the Wagner case. However, a police source told me the polygraph tests were inconclusive on some questions and deceptive on others.

Police suspect Wagner's death was likely accidental, and the young men panicked. The main person of interest, Dickie Dowell, was killed in an automobile accident on May 6, 1970 when the vehicle left the highway west of Hannibal at a high rate of speed. Police believe alcohol was a factor in his deadly crash.

In the ensuing years since Wagner's disappearance, his family has heard many rumors about his demise. "They threw him to the hogs, burned him up with a bunch of old junk cars, put him in a hog feeder... lots of stories," said Bradshaw.

Psychic Mary Riley in Wyoming knew virtually nothing about the Wagner case, but I was curious about what she might reveal if she focused on the missing boy. One early spring evening, I texted her a photograph of Wagner but did not reveal his name or details of the case. Within minutes Riley responded with stunning validating information that would, again, raise questions about the historical record.

"I haven't been able to see his [Wagner's] passing in great detail yet," Riley said. "Spirit showed me that he was in front of a building. A fight happened, and there were people standing around. Then, I see the boy in a car driven by John Wayne Gacy. I also pick up on a guy with long black hair and wearing a leather jacket," Mary revealed.

"You're sure you saw this boy in the car with John Wayne Gacy?" I asked, astonished by the new information.

"Yes, and I can see the boy's body being dumped by a body of water or in a flooded area," Mary added.

In February of 1968, when Wagner went missing, Gacy was still living in Waterloo, Iowa. If he had driven south on Missouri State Highway 61, shortly after passing Palmyra he would have come to a left turn opportunity that leads to Hannibal; continuing straight, then turning west on US 36 would have taken him to Monroe City, only minutes away.

It was a scenario that sounded all too familiar.

Today, John Wagner's name is etched on a granite tombstone in a Palmyra cemetery. The grave, however, remains empty. DNA has been obtained from Wagner's sister Peggy Porter for identification purposes should her brother's remains ever be found.

Meanwhile, the question lingers; was Gacy responsible for the murders of five Northeast Missouri boys, in 1967, 1968 and 1977? The Wagner and Enochs cases remain open with the Monroe City Police Department.

More mystery continues to unfold in the astonishing missing persons saga surrounding serial killer John Wayne Gacy. Although long dead, Gacy's demonic legacy hasn't been fully written. In the years ahead, it is very possible the list of his victims will continue to grow, as more human remains are discovered.

The pain this killer clown has caused is unfathomable.

* * *

At any given time, the FBI's Serial Crime Unit estimates there are twenty-five to fifty active serial killers in the United States. But the Washington DC-based nonprofit organization *Murder Accountability Project* (MAP) offers a much different view. After reviewing aggregate data on homicides and clusters of deaths, MAP estimates there may be as many as two thousand serial killers currently at large in the United States.

Most of them will never be caught.

John Wayne Gacy's Known Chicago Victims (1972–1978)

Timothy Jack McCoy, sixteen, vanished January 3, 1972

John Butkovich, eighteen, last seen July 31, 1975

Darrel Samson, nineteen, disappeared April 6, 1976

Samuel Stapleton, fourteen, last seen May 13, 1976

Randall Reffett, fifteen, vanished May 14, 1976

Michael Bonnin, seventeen, disappeared June 3, 1976

William Carroll, sixteen, last seen June 13, 1976

Jimmy Haakenson, sixteen, disappeared August 5, 1976

Rich Johnston, seventeen, last seen August 6, 1976

William George Bundy, nineteen, last seen October 1976

Michael Marino, fourteen, vanished October 24, 1976

Kenneth Parker, sixteen, disappeared October 24, 1976, friends with Michael Marino

Gregory Godzik, seventeen, last seen December 11, 1976

John Szyc, nineteen, disappeared January 20, 1977

Jon Prestidge, twenty, last seen March 15, 1977

Matthew Bowman, eighteen, vanished July 5, 1977

John Mowery, nineteen, disappeared September 25, 1977

Robert Gilroy, eighteen, vanished September 27, 1977

Russell Nelson, twenty-one, last seen October 17, 1977

Robert Winch, eighteen, last seen November 11, 1977

Tommy Boling, twenty, disappeared November 18, 1977

David Talsma, twenty, vanished December 9, 1977

William Kindred, nineteen, missing since February 16, 1978

Timothy O'Rourke, twenty, disappeared June 30, 1978

Frank Landingin, nineteen, vanished November 4, 1978

James Mazzara, twenty, last seen November 23, 1978

Robert Piest, fifteen, disappeared December 11, 1978

Victim No. 5, twenty-two to thirty-two

Victim No 10, seventeen to twenty-one

Victim No. 13, seventeen to twenty-one

Victim No. 21, twenty-one to twenty-seven

Victim No. 26, twenty-two to thirty

Victim No. 28, fourteen to eighteen

Resources

Bancarz, Steven, Peck, Josh, *The Second Coming of the New Age*, Defender Publishing, 2018

Basham, Don, Prince, Derek, "The Unseen War: Basic Training in Spiritual Warfare," *New Wine Magazine*, 1977

Bolton, David, *A Hike Around the Lake*, Page Publishing Inc., 2014

Christenson, Evelyn, *Battling the Price of Darkness*, Evelyn Christenson Ministry, 2010

Constable, Burt, "Man says he could have been John Wayne Gacy's first victim," *The Daily Herald* (Arlington Heights, Illinois), May 5, 2018

Disciple's Study Bible, New International Version, Cornerstone Bible Publishers

Gaudette, Emily, "How Many Serial Killers Are In The United States?," *Newsweek*, November 21, 2017

Graham, Billy, *The Classic Writings of Billy Graham*, Inspirational Press, 2004

Karras, William, Yokum, Gregory 'Tex,' *Speleological Society of America Hannibal Cave Search After-Action Report*, 1967

Kendall, R.T., "5 Facts About Demon Possession," *Charisma* magazine, September 2018

Kneeland, Douglas E., "Suspect in Mass Deaths Is Puzzle to All," *New York Times*, January 10, 1979

Linedecker, Clifford, *The Man Who Killed Boys*, St. Martin's Paperbacks, 1993

MacNutt, Francis, *Deliverance from Evil Spirits*, Baker Publishing Group, 1995

Maloney, Chris, *Unfinished Nightmare: The Search for More Victims of John Wayne Gacy*, shadowreports.com, February 7, 2011

Maples, Rajah, *Monroe City man still missing after 42 years*, KHQA-TV, February 18, 2010

Morrison, Helen, M.D., Goldberg, Harold, *My Life Among the Serial Killers: Inside the Minds of the World's Most Notorious Murderers*, William Morrow, 2004

Peale, Norman Vincent, *The Power of Positive Thinking*, Prentice Hall Press, 1952

Pearson, Rick, "State Suing to Recover Cash from Gacy Artwork," *Chicago Tribune*, October 6, 1993

Piper, John, *Jesus vs the Occult sermon, desiringgod.com*, July 26, 1981

Rignall, Jeffrey, Wilder, Ron, *29 Below: An Encounter with John Wayne Gacy*, Wellington Press, 1979

Sullivan, Terry, Maiken, Peter, *Killer Clown: The John Wayne Gacy Murders*, Pinnacle Books, 1983

Wingate, John, *Lost Boys of Hannibal: Inside America's Largest Cave Search*, Calumet Editions, 2017

Wolf, Tom, *John Wayne Gacy and the Birth of the Murderabilia Industry*, wearethemutants.com, September 2018

Acknowledgements

After a most remarkable year-long investigation, I remain deeply grateful to many individuals who assisted in the telling of this shocking story. A special thanks to Mary Riley, Britney Buckwalter and Cat Hunt for coming forward and sharing what they sensed from the unknown realm. Normally private people, they did so with the understanding they would be relinquishing a portion of their privacy in the process. They generously shared of their time to help me better understand the mysteries of this etheric, non-physical portion of God's creation, much of it still unfathomable. Foremost in their minds, always, was the well-being of the lost boys' families and our shared desire to locate three bodies and bring closure to a fifty-two-year mystery in historic Hannibal, Missouri.

A special thanks to Pastor Fred Thoni who patiently explained and wisely guided me through the process of better understanding the biblical implications of what these mediums discovered. I am grateful for his counsel and prayers as I went through the looking glass and explored these paranormal trails, while he had my back as a prayer partner.

I required law enforcement expertise in the process of writing this book. I'm grateful for FBI-trained cold case investigator Regina Webb-Bradshaw. The information Gina provided greatly illuminated our understanding of the complexities of missing person cases and the entrenched criminal element that persists in our communities. The book benefits from the expertise of New Mexico cold case investigator Steve Sederwall, also a Hannibal native. Steve freely gave his time and opinions when I needed to discuss an issue.

Much love and gratitude to my wife, Lynae, my children, my mother Betty, and siblings Brad and Sharon, as I wrestled with this story over many months and needed a sounding board and prayerful support. Brad was an important additional set of eyes and ears as we pursued the driving tours of the Hannibal area in search of important locations identified by the mediums.

I thank my friends, graphic designer Steve Mears and aerial drone pilot Dave Hirner, for their expertise in enhancing the visual storytelling through quality graphics and images. Long-time friend Paul Daniel generously gave of his time and abundant creativity to develop my blog Cardiffhill.Com.

As always, I am grateful for the guidance and counsel of Ian Graham Leask and Gary Lindberg, publishers of Calumet Editions, and their entire literary team.

About the Author

John Wingate, a former award-winning television investigative reporter, is a Minneapolis-based author of historical nonfiction. Wingate's previous book is *Lost Boys of Hannibal: Inside America's Largest Cave Search*. Follow him at his book blog CardiffHill.Com, on Facebook (authorjohnwingate) and Twitter (@Wingate_Author). John enjoys the relationship with readers and welcomes your messages and comments.

Made in the USA
Middletown, DE
18 July 2019